John H Welsh

Glimpses of Florida

Ancient, Colonial and Modern

John H Welsh

Glimpses of Florida

Ancient, Colonial and Modern

ISBN/EAN: 9783337155261

Printed in Europe, USA, Canada, Australia, Japan

Cover: Foto ©Andreas Hilbeck / pixelio.de

More available books at **www.hansebooks.com**

GLIMPSES

OF FLORIDA

—>)(<—

ANCIENT,

COLONIAL

AND MODERN

—><— —><—

By
John H. Welsh,
1895.

THE DA COSTA PRINTING HOUSE, JACKSONVILLE FLA.

PREFACE.

The writer desires to express his obligations to Bryant's "Popular History of the United States," and to Campbell's invaluable "Colonial West Florida," from which he has largely culled. Also to the following eminent writers, viz. :

Messrs. Fairbanks, Kohl, Harrera, Hildreth, Shea, Martyr, Bancroft, Pagafetta, De Vera, Smith, De Beidman, French, Charlevox, Lascarbot, Brevoort, Murphy, De Barcia, Biddell, Hackett, Laudonnaire, Parkman, Hackluyt, and others.

Should the reader question the writer's conservative estimate of the antiquity of Florida, he points to the fact that Professor Cope of Philadelphia has a creature which all naturalists are unanimous in pronouncing the first representative of the hoofed animal species. The animal is not alive, neither is it entire, so far as flesh and blood are concerned, but to the paleontologist, who cares only for the fossiled bones, the specimen is perfect. It is not larger than a yearling calf and not nearly so tall, and was found in the Wind River country in Wyoming. Professor Cope named it *Phenacodus Primævus* when it was first discovered, giving it as his opinion that it was akin to a specimen which was found several years ago in France (the paleotherium), and which gave Cuvier and the other naturalists so much trouble to classify.

At the time of the discovery of the French specimen the savants of Europe decided that it was the ancestor of the hoofed kingdom, but the Wind River fossil, which is easily distinguished as being a type of the same, is believed to be much more ancient. Cope's curiosity was found in rocks belonging to the eocene period, and the time when it grazed on the Western prairies has been placed as far back as 500,000 years.

JOHN H. WELSH.

January, 1895.

INDEX

ANCIENT FLORIDA ... 1
  The Phosphate Age ... 2
  The Bone Age ... 3
  Prehistoric Man ... 4
  The Lake Dwellers ... 4
  An Ancient Coin ... 5
  Mound Builders ... 6
DISCOVERIES OF AMERICA ... 8
  Chinese Discovery ... 8
  St. Brandin's Discovery ... 8
  The Northmen in America ... 10
  Discovery of America by the Welsh ... 12
  Venetian Discovery ... 13
  Columbus' Discovery ... 13
  Juan Ponce de Leon ... 15
  French Discovery of Explorations ... 17
  French, English and Spanish in Florida ... 19
  Massacre of the Spaniards ... 23
  French Alliance with the Indians ... 24
  Massacre of San Mateo ... 25
  Massacre of the Jesuits ... 27
FRENCH AND SPANISH STRUGGLE FOR ASCENDENCY ... 29
  Waldonado ... 29
  Don Tristram de Luna ... 29
  Don Andres D'Arriola ... 30
  Ibervilles's Expedition—The French Capture Pensacola ... 30
  Spanish Capture and Recapture of Pensacola ... 31
  British Occupation of Florida ... 32
  Spain at War with Great Britain ... 33
  Boundary Lines ... 34
  Jackson's Invasion of Florida ... 36
  Seminole War ... 38
  Jackson's Invasion of West Florida ... 39
  The War of Reconstruction ... 39
MODERN FLORIDA ... 41
  Topography of Florida ... 43
  Climate and Healthfulness ... 44
CONSUMPTION ... 46
TROPICAL AND SEMI-TROPICAL FRUITS ... 48
FLORIDA PRODUCTS ... 48
EARLY PHOSPHATE DISCOVERIES ... 49
  Geographical Position of Florida Phosphate ... 50
  Kinds of Phosphate ... 51
  Soft Phosphate ... 53
  Kaolin and Gypsum ... 60
THE BLUE AND THE GRAY ... 61
  The G. A. R. of Florida at Detroit ... 63
PUBLIC SCHOOLS IN FLORIDA ... 66
  Florida Politics ... 67
THE TRANSPORTATION LINES OF FLORIDA ... 69
  The Tropical Trunk Line ... 71
  The Florida Southern Railway ... 73
  The Plant System ... 75
  The Florida Central and Peninsular Railroad ... 78
  The Clyde Line ... 83
  The Famed Ocklawaha ... 87
  The Southern Express Company ... 91
STATE OFFICIALS ... 94
  Roster of National Guard—Florida ... 95

ANCIENT FLORIDA.

"FIRST born among the continents," says Agassiz, "though later in culture, America, so far as her physical history is concerned, has been falsely termed 'the new world.'" While Europe was represented only by islands, America stretched in an unbroken line from Nova Scotia to the far West, the Western continent reaching almost from pole to pole.

Florida is a sea formation of maritime origin, and belongs to the eocene period of the tertiary.

"History," says Prof. Lawrence Johnson, U. S. Geologist, "is clearly revealed in the rocks."

According to this, "at an early period in the world's history, there was no peninsula here. That is, Florida was not a part of the continent, and all that appeared above the water was a cluster of little islands, now indicated on the maps of the State as the Phosphate Belt, to which were added from time to time, small islets that grew out of the sea, the whole consisting of silica, shells, and carbonate of lime. Nature was not lavish in expenditure, and there was little vegetation, for the soil, such as it was, had no power of production.

Following the evolutionary period, the first important event was the accumulation of myriads of carnivorous quadrupeds upon the desolate spots, resulting in deposits of enormous quantities of bone and excreta, which enriched the soil and stimulated growth. Long time elapsed, new islands formed, adjacent spots became adhesive, every depression becoming the tomb of countless millions of moluscan and crustacean creatures, and of aquatic reptiles and mammals. Upon these depressions grew vast groves of mangrove, forming roosting places for myriads of sea fowl. These depressions in time became marl beds, rich in phosphoric acid. This was the source of that class of phosphate rock exemplified in the mines of Dunnellon, Pemberton, Anthony, Welshton and others of like character, though not of the laminated rock of the Archer and High Springs region, or river pebble, which had their origin in enormous accumulations of animal matter.

In time the ancient shore line of eocene limestone thrown up by convulsions of nature and the surging waters into every conceivable form of cone and pinnacle, became secure resting places for the birds of the sea. This continued for countless centuries, resulting in vast deposits of bone and guano, producing rank vegetation, as well as vast masses of phosphoric clay, eventuating in rock phosphate as the swamps became dry and no longer furnished humic and carbonic acid with their solvent powers.

Dr. Francis Wyatt argues that the phosphate beds were formed by the action of phosphoric acid upon the limestone rocks of the early geologic era, the acid being derived from the abundant animal and vegetable life which pervaded that region. Mr. N. H. Darton, of the United States Geological Survey, advances the theory that guano was the original source of the phosphate of lime which replaced the carbonate of lime of the limestone. Professor N. A. Pratt is satisfied that the phosphate boulders are the fossil remains of a low order of animal life, which secreted a skeleton composed of phosphate of lime, just as the coral animal deposits a skeleton of carbonate of lime. Professor Cox expresses his opinion that the phosphate deposits of Florida are due to the mineralization of an ancient guano.

There is an unsupported theory that the source of the phosphate deposits in Florida has to be sought in the eruptive masses thrown up by volcanoes of the tertiary period. That is, that phosphatic deposits result from the evolution of phonolytic masses, containing large quantities of phosphoric acid by water, and the metamorphosis of carbonate of lime, of maritime origin, into phosphate of lime by such phosphoric acid holder.

This may be called

THE PHOSPHATE AGE,

a period long preceding man and the greater part of the present animal species.

The next event in the march of time is a wonderful upheaval—an enormous volcanic eruption that transformed plains into mountains and vast stretches into oceans, evidences of which exist everywhere on the western continent, notably in the Allegheny range, the oldest mountains of the world.

The character of the volcanic masses thrown up is wonderfully variable. In the phosphate counties of Florida (as they are called), they consist largely of silicate of alumina, oxide of iron, carbonate of lime, phosphoric clay, magnesia, cinders, ashes, fragmentary phosphate rock, from tiny pebbles to immense boulders, and vast quantities of granulated matter, commonly called soft phosphate.

The general opinion of geologists is that the eocene period, in which these occurrences took place, covered an interval of countless years. Dr. Pratt says their history is written rather in countless ages.

Following the volcanic period there was an interval of gradual accumulation. That portion of Florida adjacent to what are known as the Ocklawaha, Withlacoochee, Caloosahatchie and Peace rivers was the home of the whale and other monsters of the deep. Abundant evidence of this swarming of animal life is shown by the fossil remains in these rivers, hundreds of tons being dredged daily, consisting of millions of teeth of sharks, bones of whales, hippopotami and kindred varieties. Occasionally bones in natural condition are found, but the majority are of fossil character. In the meantime the highlands, now known as the bowlder phosphate belt, extending from the Suwanee River to the southern extremity of Hernando County, teemed with animal life, mainly of the mastodon species. This is proved not only by the phosphate deposits extending 200 miles or more, but also by the vast deposits of bones found in rivers and ponds not yet converted into phosphate of lime. This may be called

THE BONE AGE,

an age prolific of extraordinary results, distinctly marking the progress of events.

This was an era of wonderful development, due to luxuriant vegetation and contact with the Gulf stream. Islands became adhesive and the peninsula gradually assumed something of its present formation, land and sea rising in nearly equal ratio. This statement is proved by the fact that the State is honeycombed by subterranean streams at various and unknown depths, and that the once surface of the State is now buried under eight hundred feet of earth, a discovery recently made in Ocala, the boring of an artesian well at the water works disclosing a stratum of brown coal five feet thick, which was not of maritime origin, at a depth of eight hundred feet, thus clearly indicating that at one time a luxuriant growth of sweet water plants existed and afterwards perished. Additional importance is given to this discovery by the fact that the excavation disclosed no evidence of volcanic or other commotion. "What underlies this has not been determined, but it is not unlikely that another maritime formation underlies the brown coal." This formation belongs to the eocene period of the tertiary, and, unlike the earth's surface, does not contain any appreciable quantity of phosphoric acid.

Here we leave geology and the no less guiding force of chemistry to briefly consider some of the evidences of antiquity surrounding us.

From the "Boneyard" at Silver Springs have been taken bones of whales, the vertebræ of which were nineteen inches in diameter; while in a pond near the head of the "run" are seen the petrified remains of a marine monster ninety feet long and five feet in diameter, said to "sparkle like diamonds in the sun."[*] In the State Museum

---

[*]Away down in the dark depths of the ocean, there are living lanterns that are borne about to light up the darkness. A queer fish called the "Midshipmite," carries the brightest and most striking of all these torches.

Along its back, under it and at the base of the fins, there are small disks that glow with a clear phosphorescent light like rows of shining buttons on the young middy's uniform. In this way it gets its name "midshipmite," by which young sailors in the navy are often called.

These disks are exactly like small "bull's-eye lanterns," with regular lenses and reflectors.

The midshipmite and leviathan of the deep, above referred to, are possibly of the same species, lapse of time accounting for difference in size.

High water prevented an inspection of this wonderful curiosity by the writer. The statement, however, comes from reliable sources.

is a nearly perfect skeleton of a mastodon, an animal that has not existed in fifty thousand years, which was dug out of the Santa Fe river, West Florida. Scattered everywhere are artificial mounds of great extent, on which giant timber grows. Shell islands, miles in extent, and of unknown depth, the homes of a race who built their habitations upon water as a protection against hostile tribes, and pottery of unknown age, both useful and ornamental, are indubitable evidences of prehistoric time .

It required two thousand years to bury the ruins of the Colosseum under forty feet of debris. Imagination runs riot when contemplating the centuries required to gradually bury the once surface of Florida under eight hundred feet of earth, strata upon strata, or even the centuries that have elapsed since the present surface was the home of the whale, and, later still, the home of the mastodon.

Should cumulative evidence of the antiquity of Florida be wanting, it is to be found in the forty-four foot phosphate rock stratum of Welshton, and the still more remarkable sixty-foot deposit of Dunnellon, deposits that could not have formed in a thousand centuries according to geology and chemistry.

PREHISTORIC MAN.

The first people who appeared after the earth became habitable were a swarthy race who wore no covering, lived in caves on the shores of seas and rivers, subsisted mainly on fish, game and the flesh of their fellows, which they killed with sticks and stones; and who, in course of time, discovered that a sharpened stone was preferable to a round one, and learned to mould it.

Geology places this period at one hundred thousand years, giving as evidence discoveries among the shell heaps, in which are found stone implements and skeletons of birds which have not existed within that time and are only found beneath successive ages of timber, forest after forest springing up at long intervals as the climate and soil became adapted to the species of animals that followed.

The first intelligent use man made of his dawning intellect was to combine the stick and stone into an artificial weapon; in time a crude hammer or hatchet followed, and with the exercise of inventive power other tools were added, such as the flint awl, spear head, stone celt, stone scraper and stone dagger. The drinking cup, made of clay, took the place of the clam shell or hollow of the hand; skins were used for clothing and fire for warmth. This epoch is known as the "Stone Age," an important record of primeval progress.

THE LAKE DWELLERS.

Following the "Stone Age" came the lake dwellers, who built their habitations on water, used a loom, and knew something of agriculture, as proved by the samples of cereals found in their habitations.

The natives of Florida, when first visited by Europeans, belonged distinctively to the stone age; their implements, habits and customs being identical with that age in every particular. It is easy, therefore, to associate the relics of a primeval race of Europe with those of the American Indian, and to understand that he was contemporaneous with his brother of Europe, and possibly antedated him.

AN ANCIENT COIN.

The writer of this work has in his possession a great curiosity in the shape of a coin, which is probably the most ancient in the world. It is about an inch and a half in diameter, and is a mixture of copper and gold.

The coin was found by a negro named Eichelberger on Mr. B. C. Bowman's place, near Welshton. It was at the bottom of a muck bed seven feet below the surface, in what was once the channel of a stream, but is now covered with heavy forest timber.

On one side of the coin is a representation of one man attacking another; both are armed with clubs, and are without covering, clearly indicating them to be of the remotest period. On the same side is an inscription, which, though submitted to a number of scholars, has not yet been deciphered, nor have the characters been recognized as belonging to the alphabet of any language now known.

On the other side is a representation of a man, evidently a Caucasian. There is also an inscription on this side which no one has been able to make out, though it has been placed under the most powerful microscopes. The coin was evidently worn as an ornament, as shown by a hole punched near the edge.

This coin may have been made by the same race that built so many of the mounds which still remain to perplex the archæologist, but, so far as ascertained, it antedates all nations of whom there is any written history, and it is not improbable that it is the work of a race once inhabiting Florida, for only in such a climate and conditions could early man have existed without covering or means of procuring subsistence. In the vicinity of this "find" are two large mounds filled with bones, pottery, etc.

There is in the Smithsonian Institute the petrified remains of a *prehistoric horse*—one of man's oldest animal companions—taken about five years ago from the Manatee river, Florida.

In the National Museum, Mexico, are the remains of a human being found in a flint rock quarry, imbedded in an immense boulder, which is said to have been not less than 35,000 years in forming.

Near Natchez, Miss., in the early part of the present century, were found human bones in association with bones of the mastodon and other extinct animals which existed at a period placed by geology at 100,000 years. The fissure, at the bottom of which the bones were found, was made during the earthquake of 1811–12.

In 1858 a skeleton was found at New Orleans, beneath four successive forests of cypress. Dr. Fowler, into whose possession the skeleton came, believed it had lain where found 50,000 years. On Petite Aüse Island, La., have been found skeletons of the mastodon under which lay fragments of pottery and matting in great confusion, evidences showing that the animal was driven within an inclosure, which was set on fire, and killed by stones and arrows.

Dr. Koch affirmed that in 1839 he dug up in the bottom lands of Bourbon river, Mo., the bones of a mastodon in such juxtaposition to human relics as to show that man and this beast met upon the spot in deadly hostility.

In 1875 a human skull was taken from a gold drift 180 feet below the surface of Table Mountain, Cal., in association with the fossil bones of extinct animals; while in 1867 or '68 a cranium was found in a mining shaft in Calaveras county which geologists pronounced an authentic find. The shaft in which the bone was found is 150 feet deep, and was sunk through five successive beds of lava and volcanic tufa and four beds of gold-bearing quartz.

MOUND BUILDERS.

Evidences of the presence of a people differing totally from those of the stone age or North American Indian are found almost everywhere upon this continent; these consist of mounds and earth works so numerous that in the State of Ohio alone there are 10,000 mounds and 1,500 earth works. This race may have been so numerous that as many as 1,000,000 may have lived in a single community. They have left many remarkable evidences of their habits, customs and singular civilization, but they many centuries ago disappeared—exterminated by some powerful and pitiless enemy. There is no data by which the exact age of these singular relics of a once numerous and industrious people can be fixed; it must have been at a very remote period of the world's history, but the ruins of the works, earth and stone which mark their occupation are generally in groups, though not continuous like a walled town, even where most extensive. But the points evidently intended for defense were selected and constructed with military skill, witnesses to the occupation of the land by an industrious, vigilant and numerous people, having a civilization and knowledge of arts peculiarly their own.

Upon one theory only, based upon fact and conjecture, can the mound builders of the western continent be accounted for: i. e., that at a period when the western and eastern continents were separated only by islands, the Morgolian race crossed over in large numbers by way of the islands of Antilla, Seven Cities, Holy Bishop, etc., (found on the earliest maps of the world) or by way of Kamschatka, and, landing on this continent, formed a juncture with the hordes of Mexico known to have migrated and eventually conquered the inhabitants, or what is more probable, forming with them a joint occupation. On no other hypothesis can the mound builders of America be accounted for.

Many attempts have been made to determine the antiquity of man by reference to the Hebrew Scriptures, the monumental inscriptions of Egypt, and the literature of Eastern nations. Jewish and Christian writers have endeavored to settle this question from the Pentateuch, but the continuity of the chronological record embodied in the Pentateuch is by no means certain; and the Masoretic Hebrew test, the LXX version, and the Samaritan Pentateuch greatly differ in respect to their chronology, as may be seen from a table in Poole's "Genesis of the Earth and Man," p. 90, which is reproduced in the Bible dictionaries of Dr. Smith and of McClintock and Strong under the article "Chronology." The tendency of the early church was to conform its chronological system to the indications afforded by the LXX. Archbishop Usher, "Chronologia Sacra," (1660), following the Hebrew text, fixed upon 4004 B. C. as the date of the creation of Adam. William Hales, "New Analysis of Chronology" (1809-14), taking the LXX. as his guide, assigned the creation of Adam to 5411 B. C., indicating a reaction in the Christian church in the direction of a longer chronology. At this period it should be recollected that the question of the antiquity of man was not sharply discriminated from that of the earth. The drift of Christian opinion with reference to this subject is further illustrated in the preface to the "Oxford Chronological Tables" (1835), which says: "The Scriptures were written for nobler and more exalted purposes than the mere transmission of dates or the gratification of antiquarian curiosity."

The Tower of Babel, the greatest work of man, is a thing of the past. The pyramids of Egypt are practically buried under mountains of drift. The Colossus of Rhodes, one of the wonders of the world, exists only in the fragments of its foundations. Assyria is but awakening to her once greatness. Pompeii, the once metropolis of the East, with its arts and sciences, was lost for ages, while Jerusalem, the "Biblical City," is known but by the teachings of Christ and a modern railway of Yankee invention.

The world lives in the rocks. Man in his architectural ruins. Who will say what rich stores of knowledge do not await the antiquarian and archæologist under the sands of Florida in buried arts and ruined cities.

DISCOVERIES OF AMERICA.

CHINESE DISCOVERY.

THE oldest claim to the discovery of America is found in the Chinese Year Book, in which are recorded events of importance occurring in the empire, in which is related the discovery of the western continent in the year 499 A. D., by a Buddhist priest, Hoei Shin.

The country which the priest called Fusang, was governed by a king who clothed himself in accordance with some astromical theory as the color of his garments was changed every two years for a cycle of ten years, when the same order was begun again. The title of the king is Ichi, who was surrounded by a nobility divided into three ranks.

A thousand miles east of Fusang, the monk said, the people were white, were covered with hair and all were women, who when they desired to become mothers had only to bathe in a certain river; their children were nourished, not from the breast, but from a tuft of hair upon the shoulder, etc.

Not the least remarkable of the narrative is that the people were all Buddhist, five beggar monks having discovered the country twenty-nine years earlier and introduced the religion of Buddha.

While there is no absolute impossibility in this story it is too improbable to be accepted as an authentic discovery of the western continent. There is nothing incredible, however, in the supposition that the Chinese may have crossed the Pacific long before Europeans crossed the Atlantic, for they were early navigators and knew in the second century of our era the use of the mariner's compass. The only corroboration of this discovery is the finding of wrecked Chinese junks (which have changed but little since they were first known to Europeans) on the west coast of America at the time of the first Spanish voyage in the Pacific.

DISCOVERY OF AMERICA BY ST. BRANDIN.

Standing on the hills of Munster and looking westward over the Atlantic ocean, fourteen centuries ago, St. Patrick said: "A man will arise, go out upon the sea and find a land which should be the paradise of the world." This declaration is not questioned, but attracted little attention from later day historians, owing to the fact that the story of St. Brandin's discovery of the western continent was lost sight of except in song and story.

The several manuscripts lately discovered in Europe, fourteen in all, begin with the prediction of St. Patrick as told to St. Brandin nearly 200 years later by Father Barindus, and the calling together of the chosen men of the community over which St. Brandin presided, to whom he said, "I ask your counsel and aid to find this promised land, should it be God's will," to which they replied : "Abbot, your will is ours, we are ready." A ship was built, having one mast in the centre; provisions and tools are put on board and the monks are on a voyage of discovery, of which they had no knowledge beyond the prediction of St. Patrick, two centuries before. The account of the voyage briefly translated is as follows:

"They went aboard, and having unfurled the sails they set out toward the summer solstice. They had a prosperous voyage westward, their only needful labors as they went along being to keep the ship braced up, and after fifteen days the wind ceased and the brethren rowed until their strength gave out. St. Brandin comforted and admonished them. 'Fear not, brethren,' said he, 'for God is in this a helper seaman and captain; take in all your oars and give out the sails. Let God do with his servants and with his ship as He pleases.'

"After forty days had passed they approached a land exceedingly rocky and high. Streamlets descended from the summit of the island and flowed into the sea, but they could find no resting place. They were troubled with hunger and thirst. Cruising about this land for three days they found an inlet capable for the passage of their ship." The reports of what they saw are marvelous.

Throughout Europe, during the middle ages, St. Brandin's n vi gation was a popular theme. It has inspired the poet not less than the scribe, and manuscript narratives of the daring exploration are extant in German, Italian, Portuguese and other European tongues.

Most writers on Columbus witness the guiding force and value of the traditional voyage of St. Brandin.

The early Portugese had explicit faith in the existence of the El Dorado, and kept looking for it. The strong evidence of this is when the Crown of Portugal ceded to the Castilians rights and dominion over the Canary Islands the treaty included St. Brandin's land. The conditional cession of St. Brandin's land by the King of Portugal to a brother sovereign occurred before the transfer to Spain.

The entire history of Norwegian exploration in the eleventh century pre-supposes the Brandinian voyages ages in advance of it. The Norseman, on reaching Iceland and Greenland, found relics, utensils and sundry vestiges of early Irish settlers in that region. In pushing farther westward they followed the beaten track of the Irish explorers. It is similar with the Portuguese in the fifteenth and sixteenth centuries. Prince Henry, the navigator, fitted out an expedition to sail in pursuit of the Island of St. Brandin. The Irish Abbot traveled in Wales and Britain, where he founded missions for people converted by himself to the Christian faith. He built in Britain the monastery of Ailech, and a church in a place called Heth. The former place is the electum of the Romans of the olden time and the St. Malo of our own day—the port of departure and return 1,000 years later of Jacques Cartier, the founder of Montreal.

In view of St. Patrick's prophecy, fulfilled by St. Brandin's voyage, it is a fact pregnant with significance that the Atlantic cable was laid in sight of Mount Brandin, which stands out prominently on the southwestern coast of Ireland at an elevation of more than 3,000 feet. It strikes the view of all who pass Ireland en route for Liverpool.

During seven years St. Brandin navigated the Atlantic ocean in his first voyage, and is, next to St Peter, associated most closely in religious thought with men of seafaring life. The Irish Abbot is preeminently the mariner saint of the calendar, wherein his memory is honored on May 16.

THE NORTHMEN IN AMERICA.

Among those who followed Eric to Greenland in 985 was Herjulf, whose son Bjarni, returning from a trading voyage, without waiting to unload his vessel, followed his father. Thick fogs beset them, and for many days they were driven by a north wind they knew not whither. When the weather cleared again they made sail and after another day and night were gladdened by the sight of land, which was not Greenland; so turned seaward, and after two days and nights again discovered land, low and wooded; this was not Greenland either. For three days and nights they continued on their way as before with a southwest wind, and for the third time made land, which was high with snowy mountains, but did not land. Three days later they once more sighted land which proved to be Cape Herjulfness, where Bjarni landed and made his home.

In the year 1000 Leif, son of Eric, ambitious to find new wonders in the country so much talked of, went to Herjulfness, bought his ship from Bjarni, and manning her with a crew of thirty-five men, put to sea. Leif reversed the order of Bjarni's voyage and sought for the land Bjarni saw last—New Foundland. Again they put to sea and sought the next land Bjarni, had seen—Nova Scotia. They set sail again with a northeast wind and in two days made land as Bjarni had done, sailing in an opposite direction with a southwest wind—the land before them being that which Bjarni had first seen when driven on the coast of New England, the bay in which they found shelter being either Mount Hope or Narragansett Bay, where they built a house and passed the winter, returning home in the spring, their vessel loaded with timber and grapes.

Two years later Thorvard, a brother of Lief, being anxious to visit the new land, was presented by Lief with his ship and with a crew of thirty men, sailed for the new country. The buildings which his brother erected were found intact, and he went into winter quarters. The summer they spent in exploring the coast along the shores of Rhode Island, Connecticut and Long Island, penetrating as far as New York.

The next spring (1004) Thorvard started on a cruise to Cape Cod, where for the first time he beheld the natives, eight of whom they killed, the ninth making his escape. This cruel deed done, they lay down to sleep; soon was heard the war cry of the natives. When the battle was over and the natives had retired it was discovered that Thorvord was mortally wounded by an arrow. He was buried with crosses at his head and feet, and the crew sailed away with the sad tidings of the death of their commander.

There was still another son of Eric, Thorstein of Ericford. He had married Gurdrid, the widow of the captain of a shipwrecked crew whom Leif had rescued. Thorstein, taking with him his wife (the first woman to land within the present limits of the United States), sailed in the spring of 1005 for the purpose of bringing home the body of his brother; but after cruising about the New England coast for months without finding the place of his burial, Thorstein returned to his native land and died soon after.

The next and most important expedition of all those to "Vineland," next to Leif's first voyage, was made by Thorfind, a merchant of Iceland, (1006) accompanied by Karlsefne, Greenland, who, before leaving, married Gurdrid, wife of Thorstein. With Karlsefne from Greenland came three merchants, Snorric Thorbraudson in the ship Karlesine, and Bjarni Grirn Oppson and Thorhall Gramason in a ship of their own.

The adventurers sailed in the spring of 1007, Gurdrid and Freydis (a natural daughter of Eric the Red) accompanied their husbands, many other women being of the expedition. Nantuckett or Martha's Vineyard was the first permanent stopping place and on the shores of Buzzard's Bay they spent the first winter.

Natives now appeared in great numbers, but with signs of peace. They landed from their canoes and gazed in wonder at the strangers. They were described as dark and ill-favored (or fierce); they had coarse hair, large eyes and broad cheeks (St. Brandin describes the natives he found on his voyage to America in the seventh century also as dark); but soon disappeared and did not return until spring, when they came in great numbers. But they came in amity, the time being spent in traffiicking. Unfortunately a trifling circumstance, the bellowing of a bull, gave offense to the Indians (called Skraellegs by the Northmen) and war followed, the Vikings beating an inglorious retreat before an image of a bull stuck on the end of a pole. Freydis, the wife of Thorvard, was not of the panic-stricken, and vainly exhorting her countrymen not to fear, seized a sword, rushed frantically upon the assailants and put them to flight, the natives evidently believing the woman a priestess who would bring upon them destruction.

This was the end of Karlsefne's attempt at colonization, and in 1010 the expedition returned, carrying with them two boys who said there lived in another part of the country a people who "wore clothes, shouted loud and carried poles with flags." This was supposed to be "White Man's Land," a colony of Irish. (Bryant's History of America, page 53.)

Other voyages were made, but there is no knowledge of permanent settlement by the Northmen on the Western continent.

DISCOVERY OF AMERICA BY THE WELSH.

The story of the discovery of America by Prince Madoc, was first related in Carradoe's history of Wales, published in 1584. Carradoe's history, however, came down only to 1157. Humphrey Lloyd, who translated it, added the story of Madoc. Lloyd received the story from Gutton Owen, a baird, who about the year 1480, claimed to have found it in the registers of current events kept in the Abby of Cornay, North Wales, and Strat Hur.

The story in brief is: On the death of Owen Gwyned, prince of North Wales, a strife arose among his sons as to who should succeed him, in which Madoc took no part, and leaving his country about 1170, put to sea in search of adventures. He sailed westward and came to a country where the natives differed from any people he had seen before. Here he left some of his people and returned to Wales, where his story of the region he had found created intense interest. The advantages he offered were so obvious, or his eloquence so persuasive, that enough went with him to fill ten ships. There is no account of their returning, and it is claimed they made a permanent settlement. There is some subsequent testimony in corroboration of this story, among which are the claims made by Dr. Thos. Lloyd, Rev. Mr. Jones, Mr. Chas. Beatty, Mr. Benj. Sutton, Capt. Isaac Steward and Mr. Williams; that between 1660 and 1767, tribes of Welsh were visited by them in Virginia, South Carolina, in the Missouri and Red river, who spoke the Welsh tongue and preserved their national customs. Caltan believes these tribes a cross between the Welsh and the Indians. "The boat they use," says Caltan, "was more like the coracle of the Welsh than the canoe of the Indians;" and in the color of their hair and eyes, they seem more allied to the white than to the red race.

Should the original source of the narrative or other manuscript be discovered touching this subject, light may be thrown on Madoc's discovery. Unfortunately no reference is made to this discovery by contemporaneous writers, in the absence ef which, and the fact that no trace of the Welsh can be found on the continent. the story of Madoc is looked upon as little more than a tradition, scarcely worthy of serious investigation.

VENETIAN DISCOVERY.

In 1558 Francesco Marceloni of Venice published a volume of letters, arranged and edited by Nicolo Zeno, purporting to be those of his ancestors, Nicolo and Antonia Zeno, written between the years 1380 and 1404. These letters and a map of the voyage had remained in the archives of the family unnoticed and unknown till coming into the hands of this Nicolo.

Starting from Frisland (which never existed), they steered west ten days, then four days northeast, and discovered land which was claimed to be a new continent—America. What part of the American coast this was it is not safe to conjecture, for, giving a starting point, Frisland, a voyage of ten days to the fabulous island Iceria, thence still northeast five days more, the imagination need submit to no trammels of latitude or longitude. From the harbor an active volcano was visible, from out of which poured a substance like pitch that ran into the sea. The country was densely populated by a people of small stature, timid, half wild, living in caves, etc.

The defenders of this irreconcilable story do not venture to deny that much of it is fable. It is difficult to believe that any actual navigator should find so many islands as described in the book and map that have no existence in the places where put and quite as hard to believe; they have all sunk into the sea if they ever existed. The Zeno story is utterly irreconcilable with the facts of history.

CHRISTOPHER COLUMBUS DISCOVERS AMERICA.

Christopher Columbus was born in Genoa, in the year 1436, and from early boyhood followed the life of a rover; finally, abandoning the sea at the age of thirty, and marrying the daughter of a renowned navigator, through whom he obtained the charts and journals from which he derived the idea of a round earth and a western route to India, to which he henceforth consecrated his life, inspired by the belief that he was destined by God to teach the truths of the gospel in distant and benighted countries.

With a patience undaunted by disappointments, a perseverance unconquerable, Columbus appealed to eyes that wanted light, to ears that would not hear. It was one thing, they said, to cruise along the coast, another to steer out boldly across a wilderness of waters. Only the learned could understand that the world was a globe; only the enlightened could believe that to penetrate the unknown was to find new wonders.

Wearied at last with negotiations ending in failure, Columbus was about to visit France, with the hope of procuring the assistance of Louis XI, when he was called to the court of Spain, through the influence of Louis de Santangel, receiver of the ecclesiastical revenues, who provided the cost of the expedition, 1,282,500 maravidis, equal to $3,847.50.

In April, 1492, an agreement was made by Ferdinand, Isabella and Columbus, by which Columbus was made Admiral and Viceroy of the seas and lands he might discover, and on the 3d of August, 1492, he sailed from Palos in command of 120 men, in three vessels, the largest, the Santa Maria, being of 100 tons burden. Seven months later he returned, surrounded by the barbaric pomp of savages, decked out with ornaments of gold and crowned with coronets of beautiful feathers, but with no thought of the great continent he had discovered, but of the Cathay of fable, of which he had dreamed a quarter of a century, and which was full of splendor and opulence. This was a delusion from which he never recovered, for not until after his death was it known that he had found a new world.

Columbus' purpose was to find a country lying south of the lands he had previously discovered, and on the 31st of July, when about to abandon his southerly course in despair, and turn westward for the Caribee Islands, one of the sailors saw from the masthead a range of three mountains. To this he gave the name of Trinidad, which it still bears.

Running along the coast, he saw, as he supposed, another island, but which was the delta of t. e great Oronoco. Entering the Gulf of Paria, he sailed for days with Trinidad on one side and the coast of the continent on the other, delighted with the beauty and verdure of the country and with the blandness of the climate, and astonished at the freshness of the water, which, with "an awful warning," met and struggled with the sea. The innermost part of the Gulf to which he penetrated he called the "Gulf of Pearls," the waters of which he believed came from the earthly paradise.

That Columbus had no thought of finding a continent, or that he was not the first discoverer of America, detracts in no measure from his discovery, for to him we are indebted for a nation of educated, progressive people. A world's asylum, where, before his coming, there roamed only the naked savage, without the capacity of civilization, thought of the past or care of the future. A hemisphere resurrected from the dead past, which, in the short space of four centuries, has reached the highest pinnacle of fame among the nations of the earth.

The subsequent career of Columbus is a striking illustration of the instability of human greatness, for we see him sitting on the throne of Spain, the honored guest of Ferdinand and Isabella, and almost in a breath of time loaded with chains, honored to-day, spat upon to-morrow, because he had not discovered the lakes of gold and rivers of pearls as fondly anticipated.

Leaving a colony at Hispaniola, which name he gave the new country, of whom he said of that colony, that "there were few men who were not vagabonds, and none who had either wife or child," Columbus returned to Spain to relate in person to his sovereign the marvelous things he had discovered.

During his absence rebellion and anarchy in Hispaniola had reached a point beyond control, and when he appealed to his sovereign for a judge to decide between him and the colony, the court sent, not a judge, but an executioner. His enemies had so far prevailed against him that Babadillo, who came professedly to examine into the troubles, usurped the government of the colony, put Columbus in chains and sent him to Spain, a common felon.

Columbus describes a "long stretch of low land, with tropical foliage." This was undoubtedly Florida.

Columbus made four voyages to America, and died May 20, 1506, leaving a name and fame imperishable as the continent he found.

JUAN PONCE DE LEON.

First Spanish Discovery and Explorations.

Juan Ponce de Leon, enriched by the subjugation of Porto Rico, resolved, when deprived of the governorship, to increase his fame by a new enterprise, and learning of a land to the northward, rich in gold, precious stones and fountains of eternal youth, determined to find this marvel of the New World; so started from Porto Rico with three vessels, March, 1512, and on the 27th landed at a point on the Florida coast at or near the present city of St. Augustine, and took possession of the country in the name of Spain. He was subsequently made Adelantado, on condition that he would colonize it.

In 1521, this first governor of territory within the limits of the present United States, returned to the province assigned him, and in a fight with the Indians, who apposed his landing, received an arrow wound, from which he subsequently died.

In 1516 Diego Miruello made a voyage to Florida, and the following year, 1517, Hernandez de Cordova touched the coast on his return from Yucatan.

In 1518 Francis Garay, governor of Jamaica, landed somewhere on the coast of Florida, but being attacked by the natives, and losing most of his men, retired. He returned the next spring and made the entire circuit of the Gulf coast of the United States. Florida, he found, was not an island as De Leon supposed, and from his ships saw many villages. This exploration occupied eighteen months, the chart of the voyage showing that the country "bendeth like a bow"— a line stretching from Yucatan to the point at which De Leon first touched making the string.

In 1528 a formidable but disastrous attempt to take possession of the country was made by Pamphilo de Narvaez, who sailed from Spain in 1527 under a commission from the emperor Charles V, with five ships, 400 men and 80 horses. He landed at Tampa Bay two days before Easter, 1528, and proceeded at once to explore the country.

They started May 1, and on June 25th a village of forty houses was reached from which the Indians had fled. This was Appalachien (Tallahassee). The woods abounded with game, the fields with maize, and gold they believed was plentiful. But hardly had they left off their heavy armor before the Indians attacked them and burned their wigwams.

But little gold or maize was found, and the natives, though not numerous, were savage, and harassed the Spaniards so that no one dare venture from the camp. Thus beset with hunger, disease and danger, all their hopes of sudden wealth destroyed, they resolved to make their way to the sea, which they reached in fifteen days.

Four survivors of this ill fated expedition slowly and painfully made their way across the present State of Texas through the Mexican province of Senora, reaching at last the coast of California, where they were succored by their countrymen, who had already invaded that country in search of emeralds, gold and slaves, and finally returned to Spain, heroes of an adventure as remarkable and as romantic as any recorded in the Spanish annals in North America; the remainder of the expedition were drowned, killed by the natives or died of disease and hunger.

The disastrous results of every expedition to Florida thus far had not shaken the belief among the adventurous Spaniards of the value of the country, and DeSoto, who had acquired wealth and fame in Peru, asked permission to take possession of Florida as its Adelantado. News of his intentions were received with enthusiasm, and gentlemen of birth and distinction flocked to his standard, some coming even from Portugal. So strong was the desire to go that men parted with their estates to purchase an interest in the expedition, excitement being increased by Cabeca de Vaca also making application to be appointed Adelantado. DeSoto went prepared for conquest as well as colonization, his force being about 700 men. The fleet consisted of nine vessels, and besides their human freight, carried between two and three hundred horses, a large herd of swine and a large number of blood hounds. The expedition sailed from Havana May 18, 1539, and landed at Tampa Bay on the 30th. The first winter was spent in the vicinity of Appalachien Bay, and in the spring the expedition pushed northward. In April, being 300 miles from Tampa Bay, their advance being to the natives as a march of a pestilence. The invaders marched northwest via the Appalachien chain, and in October reached Mayville—now Mobile—in the vicinity of which a battle took place, in which 2,500 Indians were killed or tortured to death; of the Spaniards only 18 being killed and 150 wounded by arrows.

After a month's stay at Mayville, DeSoto moved into the interior, finally reaching the Yazoo river, where he went into winter quarters, wintering the following year at the present site of Little Rock, Ark. DeSoto died May 21, 1542, and was buried in the Mississippi river. The remnant of the expedition, haggard, gaunt and half naked, finally reaching the Spanish colony Panuco, on the Gulf coast.

Twenty years after the imposing departure of DeSoto from San Lucar, a fleet still larger and of greater magnificence left Vera Cruz, Mexico, under Don Iristan de Luna, for the conquest and settlement of Florida. De Luna sailed August 14, 1559, with an army of 1,500 besides many friars, for the conversion of the Indians, and a number of women and children, but the accustomed ill fortune followed them, the fleet being wrecked in Pensacola Bay. De Luna was recalled two years later, returning with but a fragment of his grand army of occupation.

FRENCH DISCOVERY OF EXPLORATIONS.

In 1522, a single ship of the Magellan expedition, returning from Portugal, having circumnavigated the globe and solved the problem that by sailing westward the east could be reached, a new impulse was given the desire for a new passage to India. Francis I, of France, aroused to the great event of his time, in 1523 proposed to compete with other powers for a share of the New World, and to find for France a shorter route to Cathay. With this end in view an expedition put to sea from Brittany in the autumn of 1523, consisting of four vessels, three of which were lost or disabled, leaving only a single ship, the Dauphine, commanded by Giovanni da Verrazano, a native of France, and in January, 1524, after 49 days sailing, reached a new country, in the latitude of Cape Fear.

Sailing leisurely along the coast they finally reached a country of broad palms, forests of various foliage and color, festooned with vines, a verdant land, fragrant with wild roses, violets and lillies, watered by many lakes and streams, beasts of the chase, birds of gay plumage, and song birds innumerable, the balmy air of summer blowing gently on the long stretch of coast with neither rocks or hidden dangers to vex the mariner, the natives being humane and hospitable.

A few years later, France sent out another expedition, the enterprise being entrusted to Jacques Cartier, which sailed from the port of St. Malo in April, 1534, touched the coast of Newfoundland, crossed the gulf and entered a bay, which, because of its heat, he c. lled the Bay of Chaleur. The natives wore no clothes, subsisted on fish and flesh, and lived under their upturned canoes. The country was inviting, and he took possession of it in the name of the King of France.

Cartier remained but a short time, returning to St. Malo in September after an absence of a little more than four months.

Meanwhile the Reformation took deeper root in France, many were anxious to escape. Coligny proposed colonization in the New World, and in February, 1562, sent out from Havre, in the name of the King, two ships in command of Capt. John Ribault, to "discover and view a certain long coast of the West India, called La Florida."

Ribault had under his command, besides the seaman, a band of soldiers and a number of gentlemen.

The voyage was tempestuous and long, but on the 30th of April they struck "a fare coast, stretching of a great length, covered with an infinite number of fayre trees, without any hills," in the latitude of 29½ degrees, casting anchor at Matanzas Inlet, entering the St. John's river the following day, which is described as "boiling and roaring through the multitude of all kinds of fish." It was a safe and pleasant harbor; the Indians, running along the lands, welcomed them, and "showed by their gestures they were all gentleness and amitie." Some looking-glasses and other pretty things were exchanged for skins and girdles, as well cured and colored as was possible. The chief King made an oration, eloquent but unintelligible, and the French gave thanks to God. The river they called from the day on which they entered it, the river of May, now known as the St. Johns.

There was no bounds to the enthusiastic delight with which the impressible French entered upon their new possessions, and, in token of its being theirs, set up a stone column, engraved with the arms of France, on the south bank of the river; the natives looking at it with mute surprise, evidently regarding it as one of the strange puzzles of their visitors. They had yet to learn that, as heathens, they were the rightful spoils of all good Christians. The strangers chose to take the country for their own, for to them it seemed "fairest, fruitfulest and pleasantest of all the world."

From the St. Johns—river of May—they sailed northward along the coast, everywhere greeted by the natives with welcome. Everywhere they found the country full of harbors, rivers and islands, says Capt. Ribault, "of such fruitfulness as cannot, with tongue be expressed." On the 27th of May they entered Port Royal. Here a navy might ride in safety, and it was decided to plant a colony, and a fort (Fort Charles) was constructed. This done, Ribault set sail for France with his two vessels June 11th, leaving with the colonists a store of provisions, ammunition and his blessing.

In 1564, Coligny, having represented to the King that no news had been heard from the colony in Florida, a new expedition of three ships, under Capt. Rene de Laudonniere, sailed in April and in June arrived in the river May—St. Johns. The Frenchmen being greeted with shouts of welcome by a crowd of natives, men and women; their Chief leading the Frenchmen to the pillar which Ribault had set up, which the natives regarded with great reverence.

The next day the chief received the captain and his suite in state, "under the shadow of an arbor, apparalled with a great hart's skin, dressed like chamois, and painted with devices of strange and divers colors, but of so lively a portraiture, and representing antiquity, with rules so justly compassed, that there is no painter so exquisite that could find fault therewith."

Laudonniere, after sailing a few leagues along the coast, returned to the river of May without going to Port Royal, having heard, no doubt, either from the Indians or before leaving France, of the abandonment of Charles Fort. He determined to settle on the May rather, than at Port Royal, as it "was much more needful to plant in places plentiful of victuals, than in goodly havens, fair, deep, and pleasant to view." The spot chosen was just above what is now known as St. Johns Bluff, on the bend of the river. At break of day the trumpet sounded to assemble the people; a psalm of thanksgiving was sung, the blessing of God was asked upon their enterprise, and then all fell to work with shovels, cutting-hooks and hatchets.

The fort was in the shape of a triangle, fronting the river, with the bluff on one side, a marsh on the other, and the woods in the rear.

It was finished in a few days with the aid of the Indians, and was named Fort Caroline, in honor of the king, Charles XI of France.

FRENCH, ENGLISH AND SPANISH IN FLORIDA.

MASSACRE OF THE FRENCH.

Discontent and insubordination, resulting from disappointment in extravagant expectations, prevailed in Fort Caroline. LaRouquette and Guere conspired to do away with Laudonniere by mixing arsenic with his food. Another plan was to explode a keg of gunpowder under his bed; before either proposition could be carried out, the plot was discovered and the conspirators punished and sent back to France. But the spirit of discontent still remained, and soon after two small vessels were stolen by the malcontents. who made for the West India Islands on a piratical cruise. Two other vessels were speedily constructed, but when ready for sea were seized; this time the mutineers being strong enough to imprison Laudonniere and compel him to sign a roving commission authorizing them to make a cruise among the Spanish colonies, where by robbing churches and sezing treasure ships, they hoped to enrich themselves. But they soon quarreled over the booty, and three of the vessels finally fell into the hands of the Spaniards, the fourth in time returning to Fort Caroline, where Laudonniere seized the ringleaders and punished them with death.

On August 3, 1565, the French were gladdened by the sight of an English fleet commanded by Sir. John Hawkins, returning from a successful voyage to the coast of Guinea, where he had learned three years before that "stores of negroes might be had," and they were "very good merchandise in Hispaniola." Hawkins took pity on the French colony and relieved their wants. One of the English vessels was purchased and provisioned for a voyage to France, but on the 28th another fleet hove in sight—seven ships in all—which proved to be the long expected aid from France, under command of Ribault himself, empowered to supersede Laudonnierre, who was ordered home to answer charges of unwarrantable assumption of power and cruelty.

A week has passed when a third fleet appeared silently and suddenly at the mouth of the river May. When hailed as to who they were and what they wanted, the answer was that they were from Spain, that Pedro Menendez was in command, and that they had come in obedience to the king to destroy such Lutherans as should be found in his dominions. An attack was to be made in the morning. Three of Ribault's ships having gone up the river to Fort Caroline, and the other four being no match for the Spaniards, no alternative remained but to slip cables and put to sea. They outsailed the Spanish vessels, and when the chase was over, watched the Spaniards enter the river of Dolphins (Matanzas), a few miles south, and the landing of men, provisions, ordnance and ammunition.

When the report was taken back to Fort Caroline that the Spaniards had left their ships, Ribault proposed to fall upon them with all his force before they had time to fortify. Laudonniere urged the great danger of sudden storms at that season, and the defenseless condition of Fort Caroline. Ribault sailed with all the larger vessels and nearly all his effective men, leaving at Fort Caroline but 240 persons, including the sick, the women and the children, but few of them able to bear arms.

As Laudonnierr feared, Ribault's ships were scattered by a sudden and violent tempest as they were about to attack the Spaniards. This was the opportunity of Menendez, who, learning from the Indians the defenseless condition of Fort Caroline, started on the morning of the 17th with a force of 500 men, two Indian guides, and a French deserter, reaching the fort on the night of the second day, in a drenching rain. One man only is found at his post, who is speedily put to death. There was little fighting—only slaughter. Neither sex nor age were spared, according to the French account, though the Spaniards declare that quarter was given to the women and to children under the age of fifteen. All were hanged a few hours later. Over their heads Menendez put this inscription: "I do this not as to Frenchmen, but as to Lutherans." The whole number thus massacred in the name of religion was one hundred and forty-two. Those who escaped, including Laudonniere, made their way through the marshes to two little vessels Ribault had left behind him, and sailed for France without waiting for tidings of the expedition to the river of Dolphins.

Thus far Menendez was crowned with complete success; not a heretic Frenchman was left alive on the river May, and that not even the memory of them might remain the name of the river was changed to San Mateo, the nearest saint's day, that of St. Matthew, being on the 21st day of September.

Taking fifty soldiers with him, Menendez returned to his

encampment at mouth of the river of Dolphins, where the Adelantado and his followers knelt before and kissed the cross, giving thanks to God that He had enabled them to extirpate His enemies and theirs.

The next anxiety of Menendez was to know what had become of Ribault and his ships; nor had he long to wait. Intelligence was brought by the Indians that the Frenchmen were wrecked at Anastasia Island, and proceeding thither with fifty followers he found about 200 men, to whom he made himself known. Exhausted from want of food and rest and with no means of escape or subsistence, they appealed to his humanity to aid them in reaching a place of refuge at their fort—Caroline. Were they Catholics or Lutherans? he asked. They replied that they were all of the reformed religion. Then he told them that their fort was destroyed and all of the men put to the sword. As to themselves, he said that being of the new faith he "held them as enemies." They begged for shelter until succor could come to them from France. His answer was: They must give up their arms and place themselves under his mercy. Then they offered fifty thousand ducats to spare their lives, but he was inexorable, and they, not knowing how small his force was, accepted the only alternative that seemed to be left them and surrendered, giving up their arms and standards.

An inlet divided the two parties, and the Spaniards ordered that the Frenchmen should be brought over in squads of ten. As each party arrived they were led behind a sandhill out of sight of their companions. When towards night all were gathered they were again asked if they were Catholics. A dozen who professed to be Catholics and four others, carpenters and caulkers, whose services were needed, were spared, the rest were inhumanly murdered.

A cruel and inexorable fate seemed to pursue the wretched Frenchmen. The sands could scarcely have soaked up the blood of the men so treacherously murdered when Ribault himself with the rest of his followers arrived on the spot whence the others had been betrayed to their death. Menendez hurried back to the inlet. As before, he made such disposition of his men as to completely deceive the French as to his numbers, who, knowing nothing of what had transpired, asked for aid to enable them to reach Fort Caroline. The answer was that the fort had been taken and its people put to the sword; and to convince Ribault that he was completely at their mercy he was led aside and shown the pile of his murdered countrymen, still unburied. A hundred thousand ducats were offered for their lives, and they had, or thought they had a pledge for safety. The Spanish narrative asserts that no such pledge was given, while the French declare Menendez bound himself to spare their lives; but at best the answer was equivocal and meant to betray. Of the three hundred Frenchmen one hundred and fifty, with Ribault at their head, surrendered. The rest refused and went southward.

The stratagems of the previous day were again resorted to. All were led across the ridge bound as on the day before. The question was asked, were they Catholics or Lutherans? Ribault answered that all were of the reformed church. Two youths and the fifers, trumpeters and drummers were spared. The rest were put to the sword, "judging this," says Menendez in his letter to the king, "to be expedient for the services of God, our Lord, and of your majesty."

There were nearly two hundred Frenchmen still in Florida. These were soon heard of at a point down the coast (Matanzas inlet), entrenched behind temporary works, and thither the Adelantado marched against them. Most of the men surrendered on promise of safety, but a score of them escaped to the woods, declaring they would rather be eaten by savages than trust themselves to any pledge of Spanish faith.

Menendez, probably satiated with blood, did not think the immolation of the heretics who now surrendered necessary to the glory of God, nor was their number sufficient to excite any fear for the safety of his colony. These prisoners he held, therefore, to the order of the king instead of assassinating them the moment they were in his power. And the king wrote in reply: "As to those he (the Adalantado) has killed he has done well, and as to those he has saved they shall be sent to the galleys."

The heretics being all, or nearly all, killed or prisoners, Menendez had time to look after his colony at the mouth of the river of Dolphins (the present Matanzas). He had landed at this spot on the the 8th of September, after his unsuccessful chase of the French ships from the river of May. Taking possession in the name of Spain, he began the construction of a fort aided by the Indians, who treated them with great kindness, the chief—Seloove—giving them a house for immediate shelter. This was the first permanent settlement of Europeans within the present boundaries of the United States and was called St. Augustine, because on the festival day of that saint— the 28th day of August—the Spanish fleet had come in sight of the coast of Florida and run into the mouth of the river.

Not a month had elapsed since the fleet of Ribault sailed into the river of May (St. Johns). Of the French fleet but two ships were now afloat—those carrying Laudonniere and his companions back to France. Of the people the few who were alive and not prisoners were fugitives in the woods of Florida. Eight hundred Frenchmen had perished, most of them stabbed to death with their hands tied behind their backs, and the Spanish were for the time being in undisputed possession. But there was yet to come another act in the bloody baptism of the first permanent colony planted in the New World north of the Gulf of Mexico.

MASSACRE OF THE SPANIARDS.

The news of the atrocities committed by Menendez was long in reaching Europe. The horror and indignation which these tales excited were not confined to the friends and families of those who had fallen victims to treachery and cruelty, or to those who shared their sorrows from religious sympathy. But the king of France took no steps to assert the honor of the crown or the rights of the people, either by punishing the perpetrators of so horrible an outrage or by demanding that Spain bring them to justice. If vengeance or honor demanded retaliation it was left to whomsoever might take it upon himself to inflict it.

DOMINIQUE D'GOURGUES APPEARS IN RIVER OF MAY.

Nearly three years passed away, and the Spaniards in Florida had in all probability dismissed all fear of retribution for their treachery and cruelty. In the spring of 1568 three small vessels appeared off the mouth of the river of May—its name changed to San Mateo—and the garrisons of two forts, built there after the capture of Fort Caroline, saluted the strangers as they passed, supposing them to be Spanish. The salute was returned, gun for gun, but the ships were not Spanish but under the command of Dominique de Gourgues, a French captain of the highest reputation, who came to avenge the wrongs of his countrymen.

DeGourgues, returning from foreign service and hearing of the wrongs of his countrymen in Florida, and that the deed had gone unpunished nearly three years, enraged that Frenchmen should have been so shamefully betrayed to death and that no hand had been raised to smite their murderers, contrary to the rules of honorable warfare, without making his purpose public, sold out his estates and borrowing large sums of money from friends fitted out an expedition, ostensibly for the coast of Africa.

In August, 1567, he went to the coast and thence to the West Indies. His cruise extended through the winter, the expenses largely defrayed by traffic in negroes seized in fights which he is known to have had with African princes near Cape Blanco. The spring found him in harbor off the island of Cuba, when for the first time he disclosed to his crew the real object of the expedition. Calling them together, he repeated the story of the slaughter at the "bloody river of Matanzas" and asked them to avenge the monstrous cruelty. Open ears and quick sympathies received his speech; it was even easier to arouse their indignation than to restrain their impetuosity. They were hardly willing to wait for fair weather to put to sea. Wherever he would lead they would follow. Every man felt that the honor of his country was in his keeping, and vengeance for his murdered countrymen was a sacred duty.

DeGourgues stood out to sea, after passing the forts at the mouth of the River of May, that he might the better conceal his destination from the Spaniards; returning again to the coast when a few leagues northward, he entered the mouth of a small river, probably the present St. Marys. The Indians, who also supposed the strangers to be Spanish, crowded to the shore prepared to oppose their landing, for Menendez and his companions had made themselves obnoxious to the natives. But when they discovered that the newcomers were French, their old friends, they received them with every possible sign of satisfaction and welcome, followed by the wildest delight when they learned that the expedition was a hostile one to the Spaniards.

FRENCH ALLIANCE WITH THE INDIANS.

Satouriona, who had been the friend of the French, according to the Indian fashion, was the chief who received DeGourgues. Between them an alliance was entered into with the most binding Indian solemnities, a son of the chief and his wife being given as hostages for the safety of a reconnoitering party sent to examine the forts on the May. Satouriona called in all the warriors from the country round about. A rendezvous was appointed further down the coast, to which the Indians went by land, the French by water. Thence they pushed forward, wading through marshes and streams, their feet torn and bleeding by briars and shells, forcing their way through tangled forests, at their head DeGourgues and Olotocaro, a nephew of Satouriona.

At dawn they were in front of the Spanish fort on the north bank of the May, and, as at Fort Caroline when Menendez surprised it at the same hour of the day, a single sentinel only was at his post. Shouting that the French were upon them, he coolly plied a gun he brought to bear upon the advancing enemy, till Olotocaro, springing upon the platform, ran him through with a pike. The affrighted garrison rushed from their quarters in a vain attempt to escape, while French and Indians in hot fury and savage hate poured over the defenses. In a few moments, of the Spaniards only fifteen, who were seized and bound, were left alive. The attack was so sudden, the onslaught so furious, that the destruction was more complete than when Menendez, nearly three years before, had fallen in the light of the early morning, amid the roar of the storm, the cries of men and shrieks of women and children, upon the feeble garrison of Fort Caroline. But the work of destruction was but just begun; the completeness of French vengeance was to be made still more significant. The soldiers of the fort on the south bank of the river were at no loss to understand what was befalling their companions on the other side. The woods were full of Indians, the air was filled with their frightful yells of anger and defiance to the Spaniards and it was clear that something more than usual had given them confidence and courage; it certainly could be no savage hand that trained the guns and captured the fort so promptly. The murderers of Ribault and his men did not need to be told that the whites they saw among the Indians were French.

As speedily as possible DeGourgues embarked his men upon a vessel he had taken the precaution to have near at hand to cross the river, while the Indians, too impatient to await its return for them, plunged into the stream and swam over. The Spaniards, appalled and bewildered, made only a feeble attempt to defend their works and fled for their lives. The avenging French were behind them as they abandoned their fortifications; in the forest the Indians fell upon them as they sought concealment like hunted beasts in the shadows of the underbrush and woods. In this and in the other fort there were sixty men; fifteen were seized to be held a little while as captives, and in this as in the other all the rest were killed.

MASSACRE OF SAN MATEO.

San Mateo, a new fort erected by the Spaniards on the St. Johns river, about 125 miles above Fort Caroline, was yet to be taken. The alarm at that post was intense, for it was only known that both the forts below were overcome and that not a man escaped. The commander sent out a soldier, disguised as an Indian, to learn the strength and designs of the invaders, but the quick eyes of Olotocora detected the cheat; the spy was secured and the garrison remained in the belief that San Mateo was about to be surrounded by two thousand or more Frenchmen. DeGourgues rested two days and then appeared in the woods behind the fort. The garrison opened fire, which only sent the Frenchmen to the protection of the timber. Not knowing that DeGourgues' force was little more than a hundred men, the Spaniards supposed this to be only a detachment sent in advance and a sortie was made to disperse it. But the Spanish soldiers ventured too far. DeGourgues threw a body of men between them and the fort; a deadly fire, close at hand, met them in the face, in front, in flank, in the rear, the Frenchmen fell upon them sword in hand; not one was spared.

From within the palisades the Spaniards watched and saw the slaughter of their comrades. They thought no longer of defense, but only of escape. Rushing in a mob to the opposite side of the fort, they threw themselves into the woods, mad with fear for their lives, but were met with the exultant war-whoop of hundreds of savages eager for revenge, who sprang upon them from their ambush, pierced them with arrows, brought them down with crushing blows from their tomahawks, tearing the bloody scalps from heads whose brains had not yet ceased to throb. Some few possibly escaped by fighting their way through the storm of merciless slaughter; some turned and fled back again, hoping for quarter. But few, if any, escaped from sudden death. But the massacre of Fort Caroline was not yet atoned for. The flag of France once more floated over its ramparts; the bodies of nearly four hundred Spaniards lay unburied on the shores of the River of May; but there were prisoners still alive. DeGourgues ordered them to be brought before him, in the presence of his own men and his Indian allies. He was there, he said, to avenge acts which were a heinous insult to France as they were atrocious crimes against humanity; although such deeds could not be punished as they deserved, the perpetrators should at least be made to suffer all the retaliation that could be inflicted by an honorable enemy. Near by were still standing the trees on which Menendez had hanged his prisoners, beneath the inscription: "I do this, not as to Frenchmen, but as to Lutherans." To the same trees the French captain ordered the prisoners led for execution, and over their heads were the words, "I do this not as to Spaniards, but as unto traitors, robbers and murderers."

The whole force commanded by DeGourgues, including soldiers and sailors, was less than three hundred. It was not sufficient to justify an attack upon St. Augustine, nor even to await pursuit in formidable numbers from that point, which would be sure to follow if he remained upon the coast. He had done all he could to satisfy the wounded honor of his country, to avenge the perfidy and cruelty which betrayed so many of his countrymen to death. But to give completeness to his work he demolished the three forts whose garrisons he had exterminated; this done, he took leave of his Indian allies with mutual protestations of good will, with interchanges of presents, with regrets on one side at the departure of cherished friends, on the other with assurances of a speedy return. "I am willing now to live longer," said an aged squaw in the spirit of heathen philosophy, "for I have seen the Frenchmen return and the Spaniards killed." And that no doubt was the feeling of her people. There was good will toward the French, but the Spaniards were both feared and hated.

The intelligence of what DeGourgues had done reached Spain in time for the king to send a fleet to intercept him. It was not far behind him at Rochelle, where he first arrived, and followed him to other ports, but he evaded capture.

The French king would not have regretted it had the Spaniards overtaken him; for much as his deeds in Florida were applauded, especially by the Huguenots, he was looked upon coldly at court and found it prudent, when the Catholic king offered a reward for his head, to go into retirement, if not concealment. For several years he lived in obscurity and died when about to take up arms once more against his old enemies, as commander of the Portugese fleet in the service of Don Alphonso, then at war with Philip II. of Spain.

It is not certain whether DeGourgues was a Catholic or a Huguenot.

MASSACRE OF THE JESUITS.

DESTRUCTION OF ST. AUGUSTINE—BUILDING OF FORT MARION.

Menendez, freed from the hated French, did not confine his efforts to the colonization of St. Augustine, nor the conversion of the Indians, but believing that a passage to India was possible, sent a vessel carrying soldiers and priests (1566) to coast along the bays and tributary rivers in search of a passage. This expedition was unsuccessful, but Menendez was still hopeful, and four years later induced the General of the Order of Jesuits to establish an advance missionary station under Father John Baptist Segura, the head of the Jesuit Mission of Florida.

In September, 1570, the expedition landed on the banks of the Potomac, which the early Spanish settlers called Esperita Sancta, where the vessel left them, returning to St. Augustine. Traveling across the country, on foot, they reached the Rappahannock, and finally an Indian village, where they built a rude log cabin and chapel, which they named "La Madre de Dios de Iacau," (the chapel of the mother of God). During the ensuing winter the savages massacred the courageous missionaries—an Indian boy, "Alphonse," accompanying the expedition, alone being saved.

Menendez, during the following year, returned from Spain and learning of the massacre sailed up the Potomac, landed a small force and marched in pursuit of the Indians. He failed to overtake the leaders, but others were captured. The boy Alphonse related the particulars of the massacre, pointing out eight of those among the prisoners who were concerned in it. These the Adelantado hanged at the yard-arm of the vessel, first having them baptized. This done, he returned to St. Augustine, which for more than thirty years longer remained the sole European colony within the limits of the present United States. The unknown site, somewhere on the banks of the Rappahannock, of the chapel of Our Mother of God, marked the only important attempt of Spanish colonization north of Florida.

In 1586 Sir Francis Drake, on his way home from an expedition to South America, cruising along the coast of Florida in search of an English colony supposed to be on the island of Roanoke, saw an outlook on Anastasia Island. Entering the river of Dolphins he found the Spanish settlement then under command of Pedro Menendez, a nephew of the founder. In the fort was a treasure chest containing £2,000 which Drake appropriated. The town was a cluster of wooden buildings, and these he burned. As he approached the fort, from which the Spanish had fled, "forthwith came a Frenchman, being a phifer, in a little boat, playin' on his phif 'The Prince of Orange.'"

Of the companions of Ribault, whom Menendez had spared from the second massacre at Matanzas Inlet, because he had need of them, one was a fifer, and he it was, probably, who welcomed the English invader.

The coming of the English was a surprise to the Spaniards, who, being unprepared for so formidable a force, made no resistance. The destruction of St. Augustine was the act of a cruel foe, in keeping with the times.

Sir Francis Drake had no thought of conquest, and having possessed himself of everything of value, set sail for Europe, leaving the Spaniards to ruminate on the uncertainty of human events, the difficult problem of again resuscitating the little settlement on the coast of Florida, which had cost seventy four years of almost continuous strife, millions of treasure, countless thousands of dead, and the necessity of the construction of Fort Marion—the wonder of the 17th century.

The fort and outer works cover about four acres of ground.

The walls are about twelve feet thick at the base and gradually decrease as they go upward until they reach a thickness of about nine feet at the top.

The material of which it is constructed is peculiar to St. Augustine and vicinity. It is a curious formation of the sea composed of shell, sand and lime, making what is known as coquina. It is splendid material for a fortification. It does not fracture a particle, and any damage done may be quickly and easily repaired. The Apachian Indians were placed under subjection by the Spaniards and compelled to labor on the castle for sixty years. It required the labor of hundreds of workmen for many years in procuring and cutting the stone from the quarries on Anastasia Island, transporting it to the river and across the bay, and fashioning and raising it to its place; besides the Indians compelled to work on the structure some labor was constantly bestowed by the garrison.

It required 100 guns for its complete armament and a garrison of 1,000 men.*

The subsequent history of St. Augustine, from a military standpoint, is not important. In 1763 Great Britain acquired Florida by treaty, and during their twenty years' occupation St. Augustine was the capital of east Florida, after which it again became the property of Spain by treaty and remained as such until its purchase by the United States in February, 1821.

---

*The king of Spain being observed looking intently across the ocean, a courtier remarked, "Sire what do you behold?" to which the King replied, "I am looking for Fort Marion." The courtier venturing, "Sire, the distance is great." "Oh," said the King, "I know the distance, but if all the gold spent on that fort was buried within its walls, I should be able to see it."

FRENCH AND SPANISH STRUGGLE FOR ASCENDANCY.

WEST FLORIDA.

Narvaes, in command of the four rudely constructed vessels, before referred to, landed at Santa Rosa Island, October, 1528, and was, so far as positively known, the first white discoverer of Pensacola. His force consisted of two hundred and forty human beings, worn by hunger, fatigue and disappointment.

The year previously, Narvaes sailed from Mexico with a formidable force, consisting of men-at-arms, cavalry, etc., and resolving on a westward movement, landed at or near Tampa Bay, and ordering his fleet to sail along the coast, marched his land forces by a circuitous route in the same direction. This parting was fatal, for when he again reached the Gulf, in the vicinity of St. Marks, no tidings of his fleet was obtainable, and in despair he constructed the fleet we have seen off Santa Rosa Island, bound for its destination, Mexico, which it never reached.

WALDONADO.

In January, 1540, Capitano Waldonado, in command of the fleet that brought Fernando de Soto to Florida, entered Pensacola harbor and named it Puerta d'Anchusi. DeSoto determined to make the harbor his base of operations, and ordering Waldonado to Havana for supplies, sat down to await his return, a resolve probably suggested by the bones of Narvae's horses and followers. But the resolve was made only to be broken. A few days after Waldonado's departure, an Indian captive so beguiled DeSoto with tales of gold, that banishing all thoughts of Puerta d'Anchusi, he began that fatal march that carried him through South Carolina, Georgia, and Alabama, finally resulting in a grave in the bosom of the Mississippi river. Waldonado returned to Puerta d'Anchusi, October, 1540, according to instructions, but although he scoured the coast from Florida to Vera Cruz three years in search of DeSoto, it was only to learn that seventeen months previously his long-lost chief was laid to rest in the Father of Waters.

DON TRISTRAM DE LUNA.

In 1556, the Viceroy of Mexico and the Bishop of Cuba united in a memorial to Charles V. representing Florida as an inviting field for conquest and religious work. Imperial sanction was obtained, an expedition under Don Tristram de Luna was organized, and on the 14th day of August, 1559, anchored in Pensacola Bay.

The population of 2,000 souls which the fleet brought, with

needful supplies, having been landed, the work of settlement began; the destruction of the fleet by a hurricane occurred a week after its arrival. Several expeditions were sent into the interior, one of which Luna led in person, but where they went is not known. There were in this expedition two elements, which made success impossible— those who only wanted to search for gold and those who made everything subservient to the conversion of the natives. Ostensibly to secure supplies, two friars sailed for Havana, but instead persuaded the Viceroy of Mexico of the unpromising character of the country for purposes of colonization. A vice royal investigation was ordered, but was forestalled by the visit at Santa Maria of Don Angel de Villafana, who had in the meantime been appointed Governor of Florida, who permitted the dissatisfied to return in his vessels, soon after Luna and his followers were recalled.

In 1693 Don Andres de Pes entered the bay, but how long he remained, or why he came, is not known. Pes supplemented the name de Luna had given the place with de Galva, in honor of the Viceroy of Mexico, and thus it comes into colonial history with the title of Santa Maria de Galva.

DON ANDRES D'ARRIOLA.

In 1696 Don Andres d'Arriola, with a force of 300 soldiers and settlers, took formal possession of the bay and country, built a fort with bastions, called San Carlos, and began the erection of a town named Pensacola, including a chapel, the first erected on Pensacola Bay. "Irresistible, therefore," says Campbell, in his interesting and exhaustive history of "Colonial West Florida," just issued, from which we largely quote, "is the inference that the first notes of a church bell heard within the limits of the United States were those which rolled over the waters of Pensacola Bay and the white hills of Santa Rosa."

IBERVILLE'S EXPEDITION—THE FRENCH CAPTURE PENSACOLA.

In January, 1699, a French expedition, under Iberville, hove in sight of Pensacola, but observing the Spanish flag flying from the mastheads of two vessels in the harbor and the flag-staff of San Carlos, did not enter, but cast anchor off the island, permission to enter being refused. After the refusal of the Spaniards a fleet of three vessels under command of Lemdine d'Iberville, accompanied by his brothers Bienville and Sanville, taking out a colony for the settlement of Louisiana, sailed westward and took formal possession of the country west of the Perdido river. Iberville's first settlement was made at Biloxi, February 27, 1699, but was removed to Mobile in 1702.

So intimate, says Campbell, were the relations between the two colonies, that Iberville coming from France in 1702, with two war ships with succor for the French colonists, terminated his voyage at Pensacola and thence sent his supplies to Mobile in small vessels, and again in 1703 began a voyage to France by sailing from Pensacola.

On the 13th of April, 1719, two French vessels brought the French colony the intelligence that in the previous December France had declared war against Spain, an event of which the then governor of Pensacola, Don Juan Pedro Metamoras, had no knowledge. Bienville at once organized for the capture of Pensacola, and on the 5th of May attacked by land and sea. There was nothing for Metamoras but surrender, which he did with the honors of war, and was sent to Havana in French vessels. The property of the soldiers and inhabitants was respected.

SPANISH CAPTURE AND RECAPTURE OF PENSACOLA.

The French vessels, the Touloure and Mareschal de Villers, were seized by the governor of Havana, who at once determined upon the recapture of Pensacola, and accordingly sent a fleet of nine war ships and the two French vessels. In this fleet Metamoras and his lately captured troops besides others, embarked for Pensacola, and on the 6th of August entered the harbor, the French vessels flying the French flag. An armistice of two days was followed by an almost harmless cannonade, and Metamoras is again in command at Pensacola, but early in September Bienville was ready to try issues for his right to regain it, and on the 18th of September, with a fleet of six war ships, two hundred and fifty troops, besides large numbers of Canadian volunteers, engaged the Spanish fleet and San Carlos.

After a conflict of two hours, San Carlos was the only point of defense left the Spaniards, and fearing the scalping knife of the Indians surrendered. Some were sent to Havana to be exchanged for the Frenchmen who were sent there as prisoners; the others were sent to France prisoners of war, and upon the ruins of San Carlos was erected a tablet. "In the year 1718, on the 18th day of September, Monsieur Desward de Champmeslin, commander of his most Christian majesty, captured this place and the Isand of Santa Rosa by force of arms."

On February 17th, 1720, a treaty of peace between France and Spain was signed, but it was not until January, 1723, that Bienville formally restored Pensacola to the Spaniards.

In 1754 the little town of Pensacola, on Santa Rosa island, was for the third time destroyed, this time by a terrific hurricane, during which many lives were lost, after which the survivors removed to the mainland and built their homes on the present site of the city of Pensacola.

BRITISH OCCUPATION OF FLORIDA.

By the treaty of Paris, February 10th, 1763, Spain ceded Florida to Great Britain, and by the same treaty France ceded to Great Britain Canada and that part of Louisiana east of a line beginning at the source of the Mississippi river and running through its centre to the Iberville river, thence through the middle of this river, lakes Manrepas and Pontchartain to the Gulf. The British North American empire extended from the Gulf of Mexico to the Arctic sea, and on the 7th of October, 1763, by royal proclamation, the governments of East and West Florida, of which Pensacola became the capital, were established. At this time Pensacola was a straggling hamlet of forty huts. Johnstone was the first Governor of West Florida and Grant the first Governor of East Florida, both Scotchmen, a fact that gave great offense in England and caused widespread dissatisfaction among the colonists.

When the governments of West and East Florida were established, their governors were, severally, vested with authority to call for the election of General Assemblies by the people, and in 1773 issued writs accordingly, fixing the time, voting precincts and qualifications of voters, including the number of assembly-men to be chosen and day of sitting of the General Assembly at Pensacola.

The writs fixed the terms of assembly-men at three years, a provision which proved fatal to this first attempt to establish representative government in Florida. The people hailed with pleasure the approach of popular government, but opposed long terms of office. But what Governor Chester failed to accomplish in West Florida the reluctant efforts of Governor Tonyn achieved in East Florida. In 1780, the latter, against his own wishes and solely at the solicitation of others, called for the election of a General Assembly. The call having been promptly obeyed, the first representative body in Florida met in St. Augustine, January, 1781, the capital of the eastern province. This was an era of great prosperity to St. Augustine and Pensacola, the latter having a population of 25,000, many of whom, however, were slaves.

SPAIN AT WAR WITH GREAT BRITAIN.

SPAIN RECOGNIZES THE INDEPENDENCE OF THE UNITED STATES—
EVENTS IN FLORIDA—SPANIARDS CAPTURE PENSACOLA.

In 1778 the British government anticipating the alliance of Spain and France, ordered General Clinton to reinforce west Florida, and General John Campbell was sent to Pensacola with a force of 1,200 men. They did not arrive, however, until January 29, 1779. On June 16th the Spanish minister departed from London without taking his leave. Spain thereupon became an ally of France, and under the influence of the court of Versailles.

Don Bernardo de Galvez, Governor of Louisiana, on June 19th, published at New Orleans the proclamation of the Spanish king acknowledging the independence of the United States.

Galvez at once began preparations for offensive operations against forts Bute and Baton Rouge. General Campbell's first intimation of operations was the news of their capture.

In the beginning of March, 1780, Galvez advanced against Fort Charlotte, which, although forced to capitulate, made such a gallant defense that Galvez probably concluded he was not strong enough to attack Pensacola and made no further move until he had procured from Havana a large additional force and heavy artillery; but in February, 1781, advanced against the place with a large fleet and 15,000 men. The British force numbered about 1,000 regulars, besides some provincials and savages of the Creek, Choctaw and Chickasaw tribes.

In the latter months of 1780 Pensacola and the garrison of Fort George (a quadruple with bastions at each corner in which were the magazine and barracks for the garrison,) were on the point of starvation, all the resources of the British government being required for the great struggle with the armies of Washington on the Atlantic coast. Galvez's conquest had also cut off the customary supplies from the rich country lying between Mobile and the Mississippi.

But want was changed to abundance. A British cruiser captured in the gulf a number of merchant vessel loaded with rum, meal, coffee, powder, etc., besides $20,000 in coin and large quantities of silver plate (General Galvez's outfit for the campaign of 1781.)

General Campbell, weary of waiting for Galvez's attack, or concluding he had abandoned the intention of attacking Pensacola, sent an expedition against a Spanish post on the Mississippi called French Town by the English. The force consisted of 100 infantry, sixty Waldeckers and 300 Indians. It was an unfortunate enterprise, and on January 9 the remnant of the expedition reached Fort George.

On the 9th of March a preconcerted signal from the warship Mentor told the British that the long looked struggle for mastery of

Florida was at hand. By 9 a. m. next day thirty eight Spanish ships under Admiral Solana were off the harbor or landing troops and artillery. On the 11th the Spanish opened on the Mentor, to which she replied until she received twenty-eight shots, when she retired. On the 19th the Spanish fleet sailed past the British batteries though subject to a heavy fire, which lasted two hours. On April 16 Galvez was reinforced by eighteen ships and an additional land force of heavy artillery. On April 22 a landing was effected, and on the 27th of April batteries mounted with heavy siege guns completely invested Fort George, from which time the firing was continuous until May 1, when the British suspended operations for the purpose of repairing their works. The following day, however, the guns were in full play. The disclosure of the angle in which the magazine was located, secured through a provincial colonel foolishly drummed out of the fort for some misconduct, sealed the fate of Fort George. Thenceforth that angle became the mark for every Spanish shot and shell. For three days and nights the hail of iron missiles beat upon it, until at last, on the morning of May 8, the magazine was penetrated and an explosion occurred which completely demolished the fort killing fifty men outright and fatally wounding as many more. Fifteen thousand Spanish are ready for the assault, and the English capitulate upon the following terms : "The troops to march out with flying colors and drums beating. Each man with six cartridges; at the distance of 500 paces arms to be stacked; the officers to retain their swords; all the troops to be conveyed as soon as possible, at the cost of the Spaniards, to a British port to be designated by the British commander, under parole not to serve against Spain or her allies, until an equal number of the same rank of Spaniards, or of the troops of her allies, were exchanged by Great Britain, and the best of care to be taken of the sick and wounded remaining behind, who were to be forwarded as soon as they recovered." The capitulation took place May 9, 1781.

BOUNDARY LINES.

GREAT BRITAIN OCCUPIES PENSACOLA AS A BASE FROM WHICH TO
OPERATE AGAINST THE UNITED STATES.

In 1793 France owned what was known as the Province of Louisiana, a vast region which comprised, east of the Mississippi, the territory south of the thirty first degree of north latitude and as far east as the Perdido river, and, west of the Mississippi, the whole of the present Louisiana, Arkansas, Missouri, Iowa, Nebraska, Dakota, Montana, Idaho, Oregon and Washington, that part of Minnesota west of the Mississippi, Wyoming and Colorado east of the Rocky Mountains and north of the Arkansas river, and all but a small northwestern section of Kansas and the narrow northwestern strip of Indian Territory. By the Treaty of Paris of 1763, which closed our French and Indian War, the French territory east of the Mississippi passed to England, and that west of the Mississippi to Spain. By the Treaty of Paris of 1783, which ended the Revolution, England gave Florida back to Spain. During the first years of our national history, therefore, Spain owned the western shore of the Mississippi and both shores at its mouth. It was soon seen that our citizens who were settling along the Mississippi would have their commerce threatened and hampered by Spain, especially as that country at first refused us the free navigation of the river. It was not until 1795 that a treaty was negotiated by Thomas Pinckney, whereby Spain granted us free navigation of the river and the right to use New Orleans, or some other place which would be provided, as a place of deposit for merchandise. In 1800 a secret treaty was negotiated between France and Spain by which the latter "retroceded" to France the Province of Louisiana. Napoleon, then First Consul of France, threatened to send an army and fleet to New Orleans. It was feared that French ambition in Louisiana and Spanish designs in Florida would ultimately prove hurtful to us. In 1802 the right of deposit in New Orleans was taken away and no other place was designated. The western portion of the United States clamored for some governmental action. Congress appropriated $2,000,000 for the purchase of New Orleans, and President Jefferson, in 1803, sent James Monroe as minister extraordinary with discretionary powers, to act with our Minister to France, Robert R. Livingston, in the purchase. Napoleon at this time found himself burdened with debt and threatened with an English war, and proposed to sell the whole Province of Louisiana. A convention to that effect was speedily arranged and signed on April 30, 1803, by Livingston and Monroe for the United States, and Barbe-Marbois for France. The price agreed upon to be paid was $15,000,000, of which $3,750,000 were claims of our citizens against France, which the United States agreed to assume. The people of the United States as a whole rejoiced, though the Federalists claimed that the measure was unwarranted by the Constitution, and even Jefferson thought a constitutional amendment would be necessary. The purchase, however, was finally accepted without an amendment, and was generally acquiesced in. An early session of Congress was called for October 17, 1803. Two days later the treaty was ratified by the Senate, and on October 25th the House passed a resolution to carry it into effect by a vote of ninety to twenty-five, the Federalists voting in the minority. Napoleon accepted six per cent. bonds, payable in fifteen years, for this territory, which more than doubled the area of the United States. Concerning this purchase Livingstone is said to have exclaimed: "We have lived long, but this is the noblest work of our whole lives." And Napoleon is said to have remarked: "I have just given to England a maritime rival that will, sooner or later, humble her pride." Portions of the boundary line of this purchased territory were in dispute for a long time. The region acquired by this purchase was divided into the Territory of Orleans and the Territory of Louisiana.

When Great Britain, in 1763, acquired that part of Louisiana east of the Mississippi from France and Florida from Spain, she joined her portion of Louisiana to Florida and divided by the Appalachicola river, west from East Florida. Both of these passed to Spain in 1783. Spain claimed that when, in 1800, she restored Louisiana to France she only gave back what she had obtained from that country, and that West Florida, which she obtained from England, still remained hers. The United States claimed that Spain had given to France the whole original extent of her possession, and that consequently Florida was a part of our purchase from France in 1803. Our government did not press this claim till 1810.

This was the cause of hostility on the part of the Spaniards, especially at Pensacola, toward the United States, and it was easy for the British, then her ally in her war with France, to induce her to make Pensasola a base from which the Indians could be furnished supplies to wage war on the United States, and after the surrender of Detroit, combined the tribes on the western frontier in a line of warfare extending from the lakes to the Gulf of Mexico, employing as their chief emissary Tecumseh, the great Shawnee chief, who excited their enmity against the Americans by every argument, art and device which his own shrewdness could suggest or the deliberate cunning of his English allies prompted; in addition to which was the incentive of $5.00 for every American scalp, paid by British agents at Pensacola.

That Pensacola should be the Creek and Redsticks' base of supplies was according to the plan of warfare formulated at Detroit, based on Tecumseh's promised assistance.

The first startling result of the British and Indian alliance was the massacre of Fort Mims, August, 1813, an event that sent a chill of horror throughout the civilized world.

Not content with making Pensacola a base for inciting the Indians, there came in 1814 into the harbor a British fleet under William Henry Percy, and later one under Lieutenant-Colonel Edward Nicholls, for the purpose of taking possession of its fortifications. This the imbecile commander, Maurique. permitted and Fort George, which had been named St. Michael by Spaniards, resumed its English name and was occupied by a British garrison. Fort San Carlos and the batteries on Santa Rosa island were also turned over to the English, even the Governor's house being made their headquarters.

JACKSON'S INVASION OF FLORIDA—CAPTURE OF PENSACOLA.

The first aggressive operation of Percy and Nicholls against the Americans, after establishing themselves at Pensacola, was an attack on Fort Boyer on Mobile Point, preparatory to an advance on Mobile, but General Jackson's great victory over the Creeks on the 27th of March had effectually crushed them, and the treaty which followed enabled him to direct his attention to the movements of the British at Pensacola.

His first move was to put Fort Boyer in condition to resist attack; this preparation was barely accomplished, when, early in September, 1814, the British made a combined attack upon it by land and water. The former was repulsed and the latter resulted in the de truction of the Hermes, Percy's flagship, and the withdrawal of the other ships in a disabled condition, after which the fleet and land forces retired to Pensacola.

Pensacola having lost all claim to neutrality, *being under the British flag and a refuge for hostile Indians failing to keep their treaty with Jackson made with the Creeks after the victory at the Horse Shoe*, Jackson resolved to advance upon it, and on the 27th of October, 1814, took up his line of march from Fort Montgomery for Pensacola, his force numbering 3,000 effective men and a few friendly Choctaws, reaching the town on the 6th of November, and sent Major Pierre with a flag of truce to communicate the purpose of his coming, who was fired on by cannon from the fort. Jackson immediately made a reconnoissance in person and found the fort manned by Spanish as well as English troops. He likewise observed that there were in the harbor seven English war vessels, which it was necessary for him to take into account in his future operations. His plans were at once formed. A force, with several pieces of artil'ery, occupied the site of Fort St. Barnardo, which was once again to be pitted against its old antagonist, Fort George, and inferring that the enemy would anticipate an attack from the west, General Jackson, on the night of the 6th, moved the main body of his army to the eastern side of the town. In this movement he encountered a battery of two guns, which enfiladed the whole column with ball and grape, while there opened upon the troops a shower of musketry from houses, fences and gardens. The battery, however, was soon silenced by a storming party, the firing parties beating a hasty retreat.

When the command had well advanced into the town, they were met by the governor in person with a white flag, and an offer of surrender at discretion, which offer was accepted, only however for the purpose of enabling General Jackson to accomplish the real object of the expedition—the expulsion of the British. In order to readily attain that object, possession of Forts Barrancas and St. Michael was indispensible, and to the best of his ability the governor made the surrender. Captain Soto, the Spanish officer in charge of St. Michael, refused to obey the orders of the governor, and preparations were immediately made to storm the fort, which induced Soto to reconsider the refusal. The demand was made at six o'clock on the evening of the seventh, and the surrender was made at midnight.

As General Jackson withdrew his forces from the town, they were fired upon by the British vessels, but without inflicting any serious injury. At eight o'clock the following morning while a force was about to move on Fort Barrancas with the purpose of cutting off the retreat of the British fleet, there was heard a great explosion, occasioned by the blowing up of Fort Carlos. Jackson, however, sent the forces, who returned reporting the fort blown up, everything combustible burned, and the cannon spiked by the British, who had taken to their ships and sailed out of the harbor. The only casualties sustained by the Americans during these operations were seven killed and eleven wounded. On the part of the Spaniards four were killed and six wounded. Having blown up St. Michael, General Jackson set out for New Orleans November 9th, which he reached December 2d, and on January 8th won the crowning victory of the war of 1812.

SEMINOLE WAR.

The Seminoles, like the Redsticks, a brave but uncompromising race, refused to comply with the terms of the Creek treaty, and on the departure of their allies and friends the English, either fled to Pensacola or to the Seminole nation. It was in a district inhabited by the Seminoles that the fort built by Nicholls was situated, and the spirit and object which prompted its construction remained after Nicholls' departure. At length they proved a menace to navigation, besides affording an asylum for criminals, and in 1816 an expedition by land and water was sent against them under command of Colonel Duncan L. Clinch. A shot from a gunboat exploded the magazines and destroyed the larger part of the works. The destruction of the fort did not, however, give security; a feeling of unrest prevailed generally.

The first act of war was, however, the capture of a Seminole village, near the Georgia line, November 21, 1817, by an American force under Colonel Twiggs. This proved the signal for massacres, the first of which was the murder of Lieutenant Scott and his command, consisting of forty men, seven soldiers, wives and children. Whilst ascending the Apalachicola river they were fired on from a dense thicket and all were killed except one woman, taken captive, and four men, who succeeded in reaching the opposite bank of the river.

In March, 1818, General Jackson was ordered to the seat of war. He invaded East Florida, and in a campaign of six weeks crushed the Indians. In one village he found 300 scalps of men, women and children, fifty still fresh, hanging on a war pole. He also captured the Spanish Post of Saint Mark, an act for which he was severely censured.

Jackson closed his campaign against the East Florida Seminoles early in May, and obtaining satisfactory evidence that the Spanish officials at Pensacola were in sympathy with them, decided to march upon the place and repeat the lesson taught them in 1814.

JACKSON'S INVASION OF WEST FLORIDA—CAPTURE OF PENSACOLA.

Don Jore Masot, Governor of West Florida, learning of Jackson's purpose, sent him a written protest against his invasion. This protest was delivered by a Spanish officer, on May 23d, when Jackson was within a few miles of Pensacola. This had no effect, and in the afternoon of the same day it was received the American army were in possession of Fort St. Michael. Masot hastily retreated to Fort St. Carlos, to whom Jackson sent a peremptory demand for the immediate surrender of Barrancas and Pensacola, to which Masot replied: As to Pensacola, I refer you to Don Loui Piemas; as to San Carlos, I will defend it to the last extremity. On receipt of this reply Jackson, by arrangement with Piemas, took possession of Pensacola.

On the 25th Jackson replied to Masot, and on the evening of the same day San Carlos was invested firing was continued at irregular intervals. At 8 o'clock on the morning of the 27th articles of capitulation were signed, the conditions of which were that the Spanish surrender be made with honors of war, the garrison transported to Havana and rights of property respected.

Having accepted the cession of West Florida Jackson at once proceeded to constitute a provisional government under the laws of the United States, and having accomplished this, returned to his home in Tennessee.

The United States without disavowing Jackson's conduct signified its readiness to restore Pensacola and St. Marks, and in September, 1819, the Spaniards were put in possession.

On the 19th of February, 1821, the long pending treaty for the cession of Florida to the United States was ratified and General Jackson made provisional governor.

On the 3d of March, 1822, congress established a territorial government for the two Floridas as one, with W. P. Duval as governor.

Florida was admitted to the Union March 3d, 1845.

Between the admission of Florida, as a State of the Union, and secession of the State in 1861, there is little worthy of note.

THE WAR AND RECONSTRUCTION.

The war cloud growing out of the proposed admission of slaves to the territories, gathering force from the success of the Republican party in 1860, and the declaration of President Buchanan who, in his last message to Congress said: "The general government has no power to coerce a State," culminated in the withdrawal of eleven States of the Union, including Florida, and the establishment of the Southern Confederacy.

On March 4, 1861, Abraham Lincoln was inaugurated President of the United States, and holding views diametrically opposed to his predecessor on the right of a State to secede, at once issued a call for troops to put down the rebellion.

On August 9, 1865, the war terminated by the surrender of the Confederate army, followed immediately by the appointment of provisional governors in the lately seceded States.

In the winter of 1865 a general election was held in Florida, resulting in the choice of David S. Walker for governor. June 25, 1868, Florida was readmitted to the Union, the election resulting in favor of the Republican party, an event that gave rise to grave apprehension on the part of the native whites, owing to the fact that the future of the State was in the hands of negroes (their late slaves) led by a few whites known in the South as "carpet-baggers," because they were alien to the soil and had little pecuniary interest in the State. This was the beginning of reconstruction, ending eight years a'ter (1876) by the overthrow of the Republicans, years of trial and tribulation, destruction and bloodshed, during which the baser passions were given free rein—life and the pursuit of happiness being but a name That hatred of the soldiers of the Union, or even of Republicans, influenced the people of the South originally, is a popular error. The soldier of the South entertained for the soldier of the North only that admiration which one brave man accords another, enhanced by the courtesy shown in the terms of surrender; besides the soldier of the South came out of the war with no political affiliations, especially with the Democratic party of the North. Indeed it is confidentially asserted by Democrats that were it not for the rights of franchise to the negroes and consequent power over their former masters, the South to day would be the stronghold of Republicanism.

The struggle on one side was for personal rights under the law, on the other self preservation.

Forcing the ballot on 4,000,000 negroes of the Southern States without preparation or appreciation of the power conveyed made the "Solid South." The so-called "carpet-bag rule" left as a legacy a constitution that lasted twenty years, the present code of laws with but trifling alterations, and a memory of the famous "returning board" which in 1876 gave the electoral vote to Rutherford B. Hayes.*

---

*There were three sets of returns: 1. The votes of the Hayes electors, with the certificate of Governor Stearns attached, according to the decision of the State Returning Board in throwing out certain returns. 2. The votes of the Tilden electors, with the certificate of the Attorney-General of the State attached, according to the actual vote cast. 3. Same as second, with the certificate of the new Governor Drew, according to a re-canvass as ordered by the State law of January 17, 1877. The Democratic counsel maintained that the returning board had improperly and illegally thrown out votes, and that the State Supreme Court had so decided, and also that one of the Hayes electors, Humphreys, when elected, held an office under the United States and was thus disqualified. The Republicans, on the contrary, declared that the commission had no power to examine into returns made in due form; that the first return was in due form; that the second had attached to it the certificate of an officer officially unknown to the United States in the capacity of certifying officer and that the third set was also irregular, having been prepared after the electoral college had ceased in law to exist. In Humphreys' case the Republicans maintained that he had, previous to his election, sent a letter of resignation to the officer that had appointed him and that the absence of that officer was the cause of its not having been received in time. The commission in each case sustained the Republican view by a vote of 8 to 7, a strictly party vote, February 9, 1877.

The present population of Florida is highly cosmopolitan and the differences growing out of the rebellion and reconstruction are practically forgotten.

MODERN FLORIDA.

A country like the United States is in the position of a millionaire who locks up depreciated securities in a box. The bonds or shares probably were bought for a nominal price out of a superfluity of capital, and have been valued at as little. Suddenly the securities begin to be quoted again in the money market. The owner of some of the description recollects his possessions. They are drawn forth from the darkness and are seen to be worth sterling gold. Readers of the fascinating notes of a tour we have been printing day by day will perceive how the American people has awakened at length to the importance of a property of which it had almost forgotten the existence, in Florida. England may flatter itself that it has had a substantial part in directing attention to this unsuspected mine of wealth. English capitalists have been foremost among the modern discoverers of the North American Land of Flowers, and appear to be in the course of taking liberal toll, as is their right, of its riches. At any rate, the turn of this lovely peninsula has come for notice and material development. So vast are the dominions of the Union that its various capabilities have to wait before their day arrives to be noticed. Florida has had to exercise the virtue of patience for sixty years. After its cession by Spain in 1820, it was left for a couple of generations as still and dormant as if Spaniards had remained its masters. It was a winter station for a few consumptive Americans, and that was about all which was popularly known of it. Native and foreign enterprise was occupied elsewhere on the North American continent. Florida, its oranges and its alligators were destined to a long repose. Their dreams are now broken, and permanently. New York and London both are busying themselves about the trans-Atlantic gardens of the Hesperides. Already there is a "boom" in the Florida land market. British land companies have bought estates by the thousand square miles, and alligators are threatened with the doom of elephants. American speculation, abetted by British capital, is content to be blind to opportunities in its path while it is otherwise engaged. When once its eyes are open it makes up for lost time. Every resource is ransacked with a vehemence and turmoil not favorable to a discrimination of merits and demerits. Were it not for the unbiased researches of reporters like our correspondent, the tremendous upheaval now proceeding in and about Florida would hide its unquestionable virtues under a golden haze as disappointingly deceptive as the Indian legends which beguiled poor old battered Ponce de Leon to his wild goose chase after the fountain of perpetual youth.

Our correspondent warns intending immigrants and investors that they are not to expect to find Florida a country paved and ploughed. Its cities are for the most part in the germ. It is poor in roads and canals. There are not many miles of railway. One of its principal rivers is a labarynth of tortuous water alleys. Internal navigation is served by a set of steamboats not at all resembling the packets of the Mississippi and Hudson. Florida is as yet a wilderness, and they who determine to settle in it ought to inquire of themselves whether they be endowed with the qualities of pioneers. With all this, it is manifest from the letters we have published that it would be hard to find, since the Garden of Eden, a wilderness so full of charms. It is a wilderness of oleanders, orange trees, oaks and magnolias. Without manure its best soil yields 400 pounds of sea island cotton to the acre. Its second rate pine lands offer without labor the finest natural pasturage. They have only to be touched to give sugar, rice, tobacco, vegetables and every tropical fruit in prodigal abundance. After the harvest has been gathered in, all they ask is to be permitted to recuperate their strength for the next crop with the weeds, which spring up spontaneously. For the sportsman there are myriads of wild duck and turkey, herons, flamingoes, terapin, and, for the present, at all events, alligators. Merchants have their Jacksonville, with Mrs. Beecher Stowe close at hand to infuse a literary flavor into the atmosphere. Antiquaries can discover a rich store of traditions, Spanish, Indian, French, British, and American, ranging from the fortunes of de Soto, Coacon-che and his Seminoles, Sir Francis Drake, martial, gallant and unscrupulous courtiers of the Bourbons, stern Huguenots, and General Oglerhorpe, the friend of Samuel Johnson, to the soldiers of the revolution and the secession. Florida is no new country. History has passed across it with steps not so hurried and frequent that one track has been trodden out by others. Three centuries are enough for the honors of extreme age when time has been let ripen. The Spanish city of St. Augustine, the oldest city in the United States, might compare in the marks of venerable antiquity with many three times as old in Europe. Social delights are not wanting. Winter Park is a very recent rival of Saratoga Springs. Yet, on its own showing, its *soirees* in the town hall are graced by three millionaires, eight ladies, a bishop, an insurance man, a money lender, a jeweler, three hotel men, two dentists, two lawyers, three judges, with a throng of other human beings, such as these imply. There are lakes of sulphur. There are fire engines. There are the normal American towns, which can count their years on their fingers. One from which our correspondent dated a letter, the seductive name of Kissimmee, is barely a year old, and has two churches and a mayor. There is, as will be seen by our correspondent's letter of this morning, the grandest natural harbor on the North American continent. There are newspapers. There is the pious memory of General Jackson. There are colonels, judges, governors and senators in plenty. As the captain of the steamer on the Ocklawaha remarked to our correspondent, "all our people down here" are that sort. There is even just now an earl; and always and everywhere there are oranges.

A fresh and exquisite region is opened out in Florida for the pleasure and profit of the human race, especially the Anglo Saxon division of it. Florida displays the luxuriance of the tropics without their essential lassitude. Men impatient of the limitations of the Old World, which includes for practical purposes Massachusetts as well as Middlesex, have their area of choice of a new domicile now vastly extended. They have Winnepeg and Florida to elect between, the land of six months winter and the home of spring, diversified only by summer. Not a few constitutions or temperaments, tired of life on the old lines, but not prepared to skirt the Arctic regions, may embrace the occasion Florida land companies provide. Arcadia, planted with orange groves, and not devoid of newspapers, has and ought to have its attractions. At the same time, we are inclined to think that Florida is a country rather for capitalists than for peasants, for those who use brains alone, or muscles alone rather than for possessions of both. Investors may obtain a good return for their money, and labor is sure to extract its full remuneration. Florida has its career, and it is a happy one. It is destined for one of the world's most favored health resorts, and for one of its chief orchards, if not the chief. Fortunes will be lucratively employed there, and as usefully spent there. For the many who have to carve their own lot in life, nature should wear, at their setting out, a harder and more austere visage. She must, like the conqueror's bride, be courted with blows before she can be persuaded to smile to any purpose.—Extracts from the London Times.

TOPOGRAPHY OF FLORIDA.

Florida is a long arm of land, reaching from the main body of the States down into the sea, until there is but a span left between it and Cuba. It touches almost the tropics, yet is so surrounded by the ocean's influence that its climate is genial and equitable.

Florida may be described as low and undulating—the greatest elevation 400 feet, the average 100. Beginning at the northern extremity of the State, the 31st parallel, there is a ridge or "backbone" south through the center of the State, finally lost in the Everglades. From the summit of this ridge, dotted with miniature lakes and stretches of golden fruit, the descent is gradual east, west and south, ending in a coast line remarkable for countless bays and numberless estuaries teeming with oysters and fish, and a tropical luxuriance challenging admiration.

To form some general idea of the coast, the reader will keep in the mind's eye a map of the State, and imagine a line extending from Pensacola Bay in a southeasterly direction past St. George's Light, Appalachia Bay, Suwannee River—famous in song and story—

Clear Water Harbor, Egmont Key—the entrance to Tampa Bay—Sarasota, Casey's Pass, Gasparilla, Sanibel Island—the entrance to lower Charlotte Harbor and the Caloosahatchee River—Boca Ciega, Cape Romano, Ponce de Leon and Key West, the southern extremity, where an abrupt turn is made to the eastward, gradually tending northwest, past Cary's Fort Light, Biscayne Bay, New River, Hillsborough Bar and Hypoluxi, from which point to Jupiter Inlet, Waveland, Eden, Indian River Pass and Cape Canaverel, the trend is northward by west, where the counter of the shore again changes, and then on, via False Cape, Matanzas—the scene of the bloody massacre of the French—Anastasia Island—the entrance to St. Augustine—Pablo, Mayport, Fernandina—the first landing place of De Leon—Fort Clinch and Cumberland Sound, there is little change in the general direction. Here we pause, having made a tour of the coast from the Alabama line on the Gulf to the Georgia line on the Atlantic, a distance of 1,500 miles, counting bays, estuaries and inlets, a greater area of water front and more harbors than is possessed by any State of the Union or any country of Europe.

Florida embraces 58,680 square miles, one tenth of which is a labyrinth of clear water lakes and serpentine rivers.

The name of this State was originally applied to the whole neighboring region in 1512 by Ponce de Leon, who discovered it on Easter Sunday (in Spanish *Pasqua Florida*, or the Feast of Flowers). It is sometimes popularly known as the Peninsula State.

CLIMATE AND HEALTHFULNESS.

The conditions of the atmosphere in its degrees of temperature and moisture are items which affect organized life, animal and vegetable. Since the temperature of the atmosphere falls, as distance from the equator increases, one degree of depression to every added degree of latitude, and since, moreover, the thermometer falls one degree for every three hundred feet in altitude, Florida being so near the equator and so little above the sea level, might be thought from these premises to be very hot; but there are other influences which must also be taken into the account to reach the truth. There are hundreds of rivers and streams coursing over the surface; then lakes in Florida are thicker than the stars in the skies. The evaporation from these streams and lakes and from the Gulf hard by on the one side, and the Atlantic on the other, rapidly consumes or absorbs the heat of the sun, and this process is more rapid, because as the vapor rises and takes all the heat it can render insensible, the breezes from the Atlantic or Gulf bear it away and supply other atmosphere to be filled with other vapor, performing the same office in the cooling process; consequently, the thermometer in summer rises *higher* in New York, Boston and Montreal, than in St. Augustine, Tampa and Key West. Sun-stroke, with its terrors, so frequent in the cities, and, indeed, in the country north, is *never* known in Florida.

Another item to be taken in account when searching for the causes of higher temperature in summer of places north of Florida, is the fact that the days in summer are longer as we proceed northward, and the nights are shorter. There is, consequently, less time for throwing off or radiating the heat from the sun during the day until his return with new supplies.

The rainy season in Florida is in the summer months, when the showers cool the atmosphere and refresh the crops. During these months the average moisture is slightly greater than in the States further north. Observation and experiment show, however, that the humidity of Florida in summer is only 1.07 greater than that of Minnesota, while in the winter months—Florida's dry season—the moisture is less than in Minnesota by 1.08 degrees.

THE HEALTHFULNESS OF FLORIDA

is attested by reports of army officers who kept for years and made statistical reports on the subject from various military stations in the State. Surgeon General Lawson, of the United States Army, says: "The statistics of this Bureau show that the diseases which result from malaria are of a much milder type in Florida than in other States of the Union; and the number of deaths there to the number of cases of remittent fever has been much less than among the troops serving in other portions of the United States. In the Middle Division" (meaning Military Division of the United States) "the proportion is 1 death to 36 cases of remittent fever. In the Northern, 1 to 52. In the Southern, 1 to 54. In Florida it is but 1 to 287." * * * "From the carefully collected statistics of this office it appears that the annual rate of mortality of the whole Peninsular of Florida is 2.06 per centum, while in other portions of the United States it is 3.03 per centum. Indeed, it may be asserted, without fear of refutation, that Florida possesses a more agreeable and salubrious climate than any other State or Territory in the Union."

CONSUMPTION.

Its Treatment and Avoidance—Florida the Sanitarium of the World—The Last Hope of the Consumptive.

Wherever you happen to be when the doctors say "pneumonia" or "bronchitis" (they never call it consumption) go to Florida, go at once and stay there. Settle down in the high, dry, piney woods; if possible, among pleasant people and you the only invalid. Secure a large, airy room on second floor, fill the space under your bed with "fat lightwood," split finely; make sure of good ventilation; wear flannel underwear, no matter what the thermometer registers; keep out of draughts; think of all the jokes you ever heard; inflate the lungs frequently with pure, dry air, eat plain food; drink plenty of milk; exercise moderately; let the other fellow worry and shoot the first fiend who whispers: " Poor man, his days are numbered."

As to Lymph and the many other "sure cures"—bosh! Who ever knew of a consumptive cured by drugs? If you want to commit suicide, buy the dozen or more beautifully labeled bottles your friends are sure to recommend, leave them in sight, talk sick and buy a lot in a cemetery.

One of the important questions is, "What should be done in case of a hemorrhage?" 1st. Send post haste for a doctor. 2d. Lay the patient on his or her back; apply quantities of crushed ice to the chest, using a rubber bag or oil cloth, and tuck clothes alongside to absorb the drippings. 3d. Apply a jug or bottle of hot water to the feet; feed all the crushed ice the patient will swallow; give a teaspoonful of ergot of rye every half hour, and you will have done everything possible except to drive every one off the premises who is not cool and collected.

After the hemorrhage the patient should be perfectly quiet for several days, feed soups, beef juice, anything easily digested the patient desires, positively prohibiting stimulants.

That consumption can be communicated by inhaling air impregnated with bacilli, has been proved by experience. Experiments on the human subject is impracticable, but one case is on record in which the disease was unquestionably taken by inhalation. Tappenier was making some experiments on the possibility of communicating consumption to dogs by causing them to inhale the atmosphere of a room impregnated with its bacilli. His servant, a man forty years old, and free from all hereditary or physical taint, had been cautioned against entering this impregnated room. But in a spirit of bravado he did so many times. He was taken sick, and after an illness of fourteen weeks died; on post mortem examination it was found that he had the same form of consumption as the dogs that died from exposure in the chamber.

Another remarkable instance is the case of the Fugeans, amongst whom consumption was unknown until a missionary and his wife went to reside there. The latter was suffering from consumption. She took some of the children from the savage state and clothed them and did all she could to educate them. After a short time acute consumption developed amongst these children and many died; but not a single case occurred amongst the children who remained in their savage surroundings.

How else than by communication are we to account for the rapid spread of consumption amongst savage nations, where this disease was unknown before civilized people began to visit them? This is true of our own American Indians, the inhabitants of Central Africa, and many other people. Inter-marrying, or any other condition which might make hereditary transmission a possible cause, certainly could not account for its rapid progress. Besides, some of the best observers and investigators believe that consumption is not hereditary and there is much evidence in favor of this view.

With such evidence of the possibility of inhaling the bacilli, the question would naturally be asked, how does the bacilli get into the atmosphere when they are not found in the breath of sufferers from this disease? We know, positively, that in these cases bacilli are present in the mucus which is raised after coughing. In its moist condition it is impossible for it to be inhaled, but when it dries and becomes dust, it is blown about, and it is in this form that it becomes dangerous.

HOW CAN CONSUMPTION BE AVOIDED?

1. Every physician who has patients suffering from consumption should instruct them wherein the danger lies to others, as well as themselves, for it is not impossible for a consumptive to reinfect himself by uncleanly habits. Consumptives should be impressed with the importance of a proper disposal of the sputa, and effectual means should be employed to prevent its conversion into dust.

2. Proprietors of hotels and health resorts for those guests should provide suitable cuspidors, containing a non-smelling disinfectant, cleaned morning and evening regularly. It should be made imperative that cuspidors should always be used. The bedding or any other linen about the room should be removed and cleansed before any sputa on it becomes dry. When a guest leaves the hotel the walls, floor or carpet and furniture of the room should be wiped off with a damp cloth. This would be little more trouble than the present method of dusting and cleaning the room. Most of the bacilli would in this way be removed from the room and a new guest would enter it without danger.

TROPICAL AND SEMI-TROPICAL FRUITS, ETC.

The history of orange-growing in Florida as an industry is very recent. With the first settlement of St. Augustine by the Spaniards the orange was cultivated. During the period of American occupation, from the cession in 1819-21 up to the close of the civil war, many Floridians had planted and matured extensive groves. Still these ante-bellum groves were merely among the embellishments of home surroundings, a business not pursued solely for profit. Florida produces every variety of tropical and semi-tropical fruit grown, as well as all other fruits known, and crops of every variety with the possible exception of wheat.

FLORIDA PRODUCTS, 1892.

OFFICIAL.

Field Crops	$6,948,644 70
Vegetable and Garden Products	982,823 87
Fruit Crops	4,862,355 24
Live Stock	6,130,444 00
Poultry	609,763 00
Dairy Products	1,667,697 00
Miscellaneous Products	353,436 33
Cedar	500,000 00
Railway Cars and Engines	435,000 00
Naval Stores	350,000 00
Engines, Boilers and Castings	345,000 00
Palmetto-pulp Brushes, etc.	175,000 00
Railroad Ties	750,000 00
Lumber and Timber	17,500,000 00
Firewood, etc.	1,000,000 00
Shingles and Laths (Ascertained and Estimated.)	825,000 00
Lime	75,000 00
Cigars	3,350,500 00
Alligators, Hides, Teeth and Birds	55,500 00
Wagons, Carts, etc.	150,000 00
Ice	325,000 00
Moss	125,000 00
Sponges	800,000 00
Fish, Oysters, etc.	500,000 00
Ships, Steamers and Boats	225,000 00
Essences	10,500 00
Nursery Trees	250,500 00
Brick and Artificial Stone	350,000 00
Soft Phosphate	135,000 00
Rock Phosphate and Pebble	1,350,000 00
Miscellaneous Manufacture of Products	500,000 00
	$51,617,164 14

Population, January 1st, 1894, 415,000. Per Capita Income from Products, $124.37¾.

EARLY PHOSPHATE DISCOVERIES.

Florida Minerals—Phosphate.

In 1879 phosphate was discovered in Alachua county, but showing only 45.72 per cent. phosphate of lime, attracted little attention. (*a*)

In 1881 pebble phosphate was found in the Peace river, but though 60 to 65 per cent. phosphate of lime and in large quantity, efforts to secure capital for mining were unavailing, and it was not until 1888 that operations begun. (*b*)

Early in 1888 a body of white marl was found at Welshton, which was thought to be fireclay, but for that purpose proved worthless. Believing, however, it might be of value on sandy land, tests were made with gratifying results. Analysis showed 63.38 per cent. phosphate of lime, and it was put upon the market. (*c*)

In May, 1889, a peculiar rock formation imbedded in a clay matrix was found at Dunnellon, which analyzed 80 per cent. phosphate of lime. This deposit, including ten acres, was sold for $10,000 and formed the nucleus of the Dunnellon Phosphate Company, whose stock, capitalized at $1,200,000, sold at a premium of 60 per cent. (*d*)

There are now 108 phosphate companies in Florida, 71 of which report invested capital of $14,226,067, and an annual expenditure of $1,987,374, including transportation to port of entry. The total capital invested in Florida phosphate lands is probably $50,000,000.

The total phosphate area developed is 33,056 acres, and the total phosphate in sight 133 056,416 tons of 2,240 pounds. The net value of *all* phosphate lands, including soft phosphate, plate rock, hard rock and pebble, is estimated at $1,000,000,000. Some idea of the growing importance of the phosphate business may be gathered from the fact that in 1888 the total shipments were but 813 tons, while in 1893 the shipments were 354,327 tons.

The purchase of the ten acres referred to was the forerunner of an era of speculation that honeycombed the State, shook the Nation from center to circumference, and reaching across the Atlantic almost paralized an important industry.

(*a*) Discoverer unknown.
(*b*) Capt. J. Francis Le Baron, U. S. Engineer Corps, discoverer.
(*c*) Capt John H. Welsh, discoverer.
(*d*) Mr. Alburtus Vogt, discoverer.

GEOGRAPHICAL POSITION OF THE FLORIDA PHOSPHATE.

The phosphate belt of Florida, as applied to the workable deposits, having an economic and commercial value, commences at the head of the Wacissa river in Jefferson county, about four miles south and eighteen miles east of Tallahassee; thence it extends southeast to the Aucilla river, near a point where the three counties of Jefferson, Madison and Taylor join, where deposits of considerable extent and of fine quality are found; thence through Taylor county, with a trace or straggling deposit here and there, by a southeast course to the Steinhatchee river in Lafayette county, where large and valuable deposits have been located. Directly north of the Steinhatchee phosphate region, and chiefly on the east bank of the Suwannee river, and around the little village of Luraville, large bodies of high grade composite phosphate have been located. Thence the belt extends southeast again for a distance of about twenty-five miles, with very little evidence of phosphate on the way, and Ichetucknee Springs in Columbia county, is reached, around which are some rich deposits. Leaving the springs and traveling south, indications are seen here and there. Passing near the town of Fort White and the rich deposits in its immediate vicinity, crossing the Santa Fe river and traversing this hard rock territory for a distance of twenty-four miles, High Springs in Alachua county is reached; thence due south are deposits scattered all about for twenty-four miles to the Albion region of Levy county, to the westward of the tracts just described. Straggling along a distance of about twenty miles in the western part of Alachua and Levy counties from north to south, is the Trenton region, where fine composite phosphate lands, rich and easily worked, have been located.

Returning to Albion and traveling south and east through Levy county fifteen miles to Stafford's Pond, thence on through Marion county, taking in on the way a number of rich mines in the Early Bird region, we reach the Dunnellon mines, where the discovery of hard rock phosphate was originally made, where the first mine was opened, and where is now the largest hard rock company in the state. Crossing the Withlacoochee river the belt extends a little east of south through the rich and favored mineral counties of Citrus and Hernando, broadening out and reaching so far to the east as to take in the western border of Sumter county, again veering to the west, thence on to a point four miles south of Dade City in Pasco county, where the southern limit of the hard rock belt is reached. Its total length from Ichetucknee Springs to the point named is about 160 miles, through a broken but continuous chain of phosphate deposits, its general trend being north-west to south-east with an average width of twelve to fifteen miles, in several places widening out so as to embrace, in a fragmentary way, as much as twenty miles. To the east and parallel with the hard rock belt, and lying almost wholly within Marion county, is what is known as the plate rock region, of which Anthony, Welshton, Belleview and Summerfield are the present active centres. The plate rock belt extends from Orange Lake on the north to the southwest corner of Lake Weir on the south, a distance of thirty miles or more, with an average width of two to three miles. The territory from Ichetucknee Springs to Dade City is described as the phosphate belt proper, because it is more compact and better defined, but including the Luraville, Steinhatchee, Aucilla and Wacissa rivers, and deposits adjacent thereto, hard rock may be found for a distance of more than 200 miles, in its course traversing the counties of Jefferson, Madison, Taylor, Lafayette, Suwannee, Columbia, Alachua, Levy, Marion, Citrus, Hernando, Sumter and Pasco. In a general way it conforms to the configuration of the Gulf coast, but touches it nowhere, and only in one place approaches as near as eight miles. The territory described is known as the hard rock belt, because the phosphate is hard, as its name applies, and is generally high grade, and though subject to several subdivisions, is believed to be of a common origin.

The sub divisions are: 1st, hard rock; 2d, plate rock; 3d, composite, a mixture of hard rock and fragmentary stuff, to which may be added the gravel screenings and soft phosphate.

KINDS OF PHOSPHATE.

HARD ROCK.

The hard rock belt, which covers so large a part of the phosphate field, naturally takes its name from the hard rock phosphate which there predominates, and which may be said to be the basis of at least three other kinds, viz: the gravel screenings, the plate rock and the composite, with an intimate connection with still another kind, the soft phosphate. Dr. Pratt believes the soft to have been the producing cause of all the rest, the spawn or spore from which it originated.

PLATE ROCK.

As described in another place, the plate rock field is a belt by itself, with the same general trend as the main belt, running from about north-northwest to south southeast.

It lies almost wholly within Marion county. In extent it is the smallest of all the deposits, being about thirty miles long, with an average width of about three miles. The peculiar rock from which it takes its name is platelike, the rock resembling the broken fragments of a stock of plates. The broken pieces are of angular form and vary from one to six inches in breadth. In thickness they vary from one-fourth of an inch, or even less, to fully one inch. The rock is heavy and hard, and is often worn smooth and white like ivory. A clean, sound piece will ring when struck. The prevailing color is cream and yellowish when taken from the mine.

COMPOSITE PHOSPHATE.

The composite belt is so denominated because the phosphate there found is of two kinds, the hard rock bowlders, as found in the hard rock belt proper, though in smaller quantities, and the drift surrounding the bowlders, often covering many acres, composed of plate rock and gravel screenings, as described elsewhere. At Luraville, in Suwannee county, where it was first discovered, this singularity was marked. South of Luraville, on the Steinhatchee river in Lafayette county, the same general features are observed, though the land lies lower and the phosphate is somewhat adulterated with sandstone.

RIVER PEBBLE.

The river pebble is so denominated because it is found in the beds of rivers and their tributaries. It was first discovered in Peace river, but has since been found in the Alafia, Manatee, Miakka, Caloosahatchee and Withlacoochee on the Gulf slope, and in the Black river on the Atlantic slope. The Peace, the Alafia and the Black river deposits are of the same general type, and are now generally believed to have had their origin in the land pebble, which it much resembles in shape and size, though it is generally smoother, and grades down in size the further it is found from the source of supply. This is due, no doubt, to abrasion and wear from being so often moved in great bodies by the annual floods and changes of the channel, as well as the erosion from the never ceasing flow of the river currents. In size it varies from less than that of a broken grain of rice up to that of a pea or bean, and is often as large as a hickory nut.

LAND PEBBLE.

The land pebble phosphate is a formation distinct from the others. It is pebbly, as its name indicates, is of small size, and is somewhat lighter in weight than other forms. In color it varies from cream or yellow to slate, brown or gray. When well bleached much of it is snow white and of varied degrees of hardness. This pebble runs in size from what is called pin head up to the size of a pea or bean, and even larger. Often the soft pebbles have run together, forming conglomerate balls of various sizes and shapes, the largest measuring several inches in diameter. This applies to the drift. In that of animal origin the fossils are of all sizes, from the tiniest shellfish or tooth to the remains of the sea-cow, mastodon or elephant.

SOFT PHOSPHATE.

To comprehend the importance of soft phosphate it is necessary to know the acreage in cultivation in the United States and the amount of phosphate of lime necessary to production. The total acreage is calculated at 429,200,000, and the average consumption of phosphoric acid for a single crop at nineteen pounds. The total consumption of phosphoric acid is therefore 8,142,400,000 pounds, equivalent to 16 767,820,226 pounds phosphate of lime, or 838,391 tons

Estimating soft phosphate, the best form of phosphate of lime, at a low estimate, there would be required for a single crop, if phosphate of lime was not otherwise obtainable, 1,676,782 tons, which, at the price of prepared soft phosphate; that is, dried, pulverized and in bags, $8.00 per ton, we have a total of $13,414,256.

The figures given are for phosphate of lime found in the product, phosphate of lime going into the soil, to be taken up later, not being calculated.

HISTORICAL.

So far back as the year 1698 a celebrated French engineer (Vauban), writing in the Dime Royal, said: "We have for a long time past been universally complaining of the falling off in quantity and quality of crops; our farms are no longer giving us the returns we were accustomed to, yet few persons are taking the pains to examine into the causes of this diminution, which will become more and more formidable unless proper remedies are discovered and applied." This was a warning note, but it was not until after the commencement of the present century that the English farmer began to use crushed bones as a manure, and even they did so in blind ignorance of the principles to which they owed their virtues, as is clearly shown by an article published by one of the scientific papers of that day (1830), in which the writer says: "We need take into no account the earthy matters to phosphate of lime contained in the bones, because, as it is indestructible and insoluble, it cannot serve as a manure, even though it is placed in a damp soil with a combination of circumstances analytically stronger than any of the processes known to organic chemistry." A subsequen writer upon the same subject declares that "bones, after having under gone a certain process of fermentation, contain no more than 2 per cent. of gelatin, and, as they derive their fertilizing power from this substance only, they may be considered as having no value as manure." That such opinions as these should have prevailed only fifty years ago seems preposterous because of the gigantic strides which we have made since then, and because of the fact that

THE CHINESE KNEW

that the fertilizer was a mineral principle, and for many centuries used burnt bones as manures. Despite the unflagging researches of the best minds of the times, it was not until 1843 that the Duke of Richmond, after an exhaustive series of experiments upon the soil with both fresh and degelatinized bones, came to the conclusion that they owed their value not to gelatine or fatty matters, but to their large percentage of phosphoric acid. The spark thus emitted soon spread into a flame, and conclusive experiments shortly after published by the illustrious Boussingault set all uncertainty at rest forever. Numerous species of vegetables were planted in burnt sand, which was ascertained by analysis to contain no trace of phosphoric acid. It was, however, made rich in every other element of fertility. No development of these plants took place until phosphate of lime had been added to the sand, but after this their growth became flourishing. Meanwhile large workable deposits of mineral phosphates were already known to exist, having been almost simultaneously discovered in their respective countries by Buckland in England, Berthier in France, and Holmes in America. In the course of a lecture delivered to the British Association in 1845, Professor Henslow, describing the Suffolk coprolites, suggested the immense value of their application to agriculture. From this time may be dated the development of phosphate mining as an industry, the pursuit of which has proved so remunerative to capital and labor.

SIXTY YEARS AGO

the science of agriculture was in its infancy. Our grandfathers could not understand why lands once so fertile and productive should show signs of approaching exhaustion. The light only came to us after we had studied how outdoor plants live, whence they obtain their food, of what elements that food is composed, and how it is conveyed and absorbed into their organisms. In point of fact, we have discovered that the manner of life in plants is very similar to the manner of life in animals and man. They require certain foods in stated proportions which pass through the process of digestion; they must breathe a certain atmosphere, and they are subject to the influences of heat and cold, light and darkness.

The tissues of their bodies, like ours, are composed of carbon, hydrogen, oxygen, nitrogen and certain mineral acids and bases, such as phosphoric and sulphuric acids, lime, potash, magnesia and iron. Since, therefore, it is admittedly necessary for man to constantly absorb a sufficiency of these elements in the form of food, it follows that similar food is required by plants for similar purposes. Having determined the elementary composition of plants, investigators directed their attention to the analysis of soils in order to establish comparisons between virgin or uncultivated lands and old varieties which had long been tributaries to every kind of culture. It was found that in the former there is an abundance of most of the dominating mineral ingredients discovered in plant organisms, whereas in the latter they either exist only in minute proportions or are lacking altogether. This marked a most important stage in our progress. Argument is no

ANCIENT, COLONIAL AND MODERN.

longer necessary to prove that if agriculture is to continue to be the basis of national wealth and prosperity, means must be found of restoring to our soils the chief elements yearly taken away from them by the crops. These chief elements have been shown to be nitrogen, phosphoric acid and potash, and the most important parts in the functions of vegetation, and are the most liable to exhaustion.

Previous to 1841 the principal commercial fertilizer was bone dust, that being the only form of phosphate of lime then known. About the year 1833 Thomas Graham, a Scotch chemist, had made a careful investigation into the chemical nature of phosphoric acid and phosphatic salts. The result of his investigation was the widespread use of bone dust as a fertilizer. It was found, however, that it was necessary to use as much as 1,000 to 1,200 pounds per acre to secure the best results, owing to the fact that the phosphate of lime in bones is so slightly soluble in water.

In 1841 guano was introduced from the Chincha Islands of Peru. Because of the greater solubility of this fertilizer and the consequent better results obtained from its use the demand for it rapidly increased. At this time Liebig, the German chemist, discovered and formulated the method of making soluble the phosphate of lime contained in bones by treating the bone dust with sulphuric acid.

Speaking of the advantage to be derived from the application of finely powdered raw phosphates, Dr. Wyatt says:

"Nothing of any serious moment has, in fact, occurred to modify the conclusions formulated in 1857 by the well known Frenchman, DeMolon, who, reporting on a very extensive series of trials of ground raw coprolite in many different departments of France, said that: 'First, it might be used with advantage in clayey, schistous, granitic and sandy soils rich in organic matter; second, if these soils were deficient in organic matter, or had long been under cultivation, it might still be used in combination with animal manure.'"

Professor E. T. Cox, at the Washington meeting of the American Association for the Advancement of Science, August 20, 1891, referring to crude phosphate as a fertilizer, says:

"But why convert the pebbles into acid phosphate? The acid phosphate is reverted into phosphate of iron and alumina after it is applied to the land by the presence of iron and alumina that are found in all arable soils. It is, in my opinion, far more economical for the farmer to apply to his land the phosphate of lime in the form of a fine powder than to apply the acid phosphate.

"In this case the more phosphate of alumina it contains the better, as it will be more readily assimilated by the plants than reverted phosphoric acid, which results from the application of superphosphates to soils containing iron and alumina."

In connection with the foregoing, Professor Cox quoted from a letter of Henry Wurtz, Ph. D., to whom he had submitted his paper. Dr. Wurtz writes:

"What you say about a merely mechanical treatment, in the preparation for use of these phosphatic gravels; that is, mainly by fine comminution, meets the approval of my own mind, through my own reading, experience and investigation in every way. The efficiency of phosphate as fertilizers is rationally explainable by their conversion into polymeric forms, soluble in the liquids which occur in the soil or arise from the natural excretions of the radicles of plants, or from products of plant decay. Such excrements, *sou al.*, convert phosphates into soluble polymeric or other forms.

"Mulder claimed that these solvent or transforming agents are the organic acids of decay, such as those called humic, ulmic, crenic, apocrenic, etc. H. von Liebig, some ten years since, claimed that roots secrete or excrete oxalic acid, which alone, or with the ammonia of the soil, or of both, dissolves solid phosphates.

"Gladding proved that organic salts of ammonia can completely dissolve or cause to pass into solution not only lime, but alumina and iron phosphates. Other chemists (as Millot) have shown that ammonia salts even prevent the reversion or precipitation of dissolved phosphates in the soil. It is undeniable that great mechanical comminuiton has been proved by numerous experiments to be almost, if not quite, as efficient as chemical solution in the promotion of the absorbtion of phosphates by plant radicles. If the clayey phosphates (meaning the soft phosphate herein described) you describe snould really pan out 50 per cent., or even less, of tri-calcium phosphate, with or without iron and aluminum phosphates, its importance appears to me incalculable. The mass of remarkable and significant chemical facts in the literature of soils and fertilizers has surprised me; apparently no master mind has yet reduced them to any available system of soil science."

Soft phosphate should not be confounded with "floats" or rock phosphate in any form, the former giving up all its fertilizing properties in from one to two years, according to natural solubility and fineness of pulverization; the latter yielding 5 per cent. per annum until its fertilizing properties are exhausted. Besides, there are valuable properties in the former, such as magnesia, carbonate of lime, etc., which the latter does not possess, and a power of absorption and retention of moisture of incalculable value.

The report of the United States Commissioner of Labor on the soft phosphate industry of Florida for th` year ending December 31, 1892 (from which we largely quoted), says:

"The increase in the yield of cotton, in test rows manured with soft phosphate, was marked, and proved the phosphate to be better than animal manure and standard fertilizers.

"The concensus of opinions is, that it is a manure of surpassing virtue, and for the purpose of restoring exhausted lands and old worn out farms is the cheapest and, at the same time, the best fertilizer.

"It is generally believed that it gives better results than any other kind of raw phosphate, or even ground bone.

"During the protracted drought of 1891 trees and crops treated with soft phosphate endured the trying ordeal much better than others, whether manured or unmanured."

Captain James F. Tucker, special agent Department of Labor, who has made a long study of Florida soft phosphate, says: "In one case I used soft phosphate on a row of orange trees and none on the row adjoining. With the exception of phosphate all the conditions were equal. The crop on the row fertilized with phosphate was 40 per cent. greater than the row on which there was no phosphate."

Professor Lawrence Johnson, U. S. Geolgist, says of Florida soft (marl) phosphate: "It is a natural high grade fertilizer, and a great boon to the farmers and fruit growers of the country."

Dr. Shephard, of the Charleston Laboratory, a chemist of world-wide reputation, says: "Put all the money you can spare into soft phosphate and spread it on your land."

Dr. Pratt (probably the highest authority in the United States) says of soft phosphate: "It will come into general use, with great permanent benefit to the land."

Liebig says: "Organic matter undergoing decay accumulates carbonic acid, and thereby acquires the power of taking up phosphate of lime."

TWO EXPERIMENTS.

To test the comparative productiveness of ground raw phosphate and acid phosphate under different conditions, and to determine whether decomposing organic matter converts insoluble into soluble phosphate, two sets of experiments were carried out by the Alabama Experiment Station, one on the farm and the other in the chemical laboratory.

The materials used were carefully analyzed by Dr. Anderson, assistant chemist, with the following results: The acid phosphate gave

Water Soluble Phosphoric Acid (P_2O_5).. 9.10 per cent.
Citrate Soluble Phosphoric Acid (P_2O_5)........ .. .. 2.94 "
Acid Soluble Phosphoric Acid (P_2O_5) .... 2.32 "

Total Phosphoric Acid)P_5O_5) 14.36

The Florida soft phosphate reduced to a fine powder similar to floats gave

$\qquad$ 8
Moisture 4.13
Total Phosphoric Acid (Acid Soluble)................................... .. ..16.59
Iron and Aluminum Oxides...... .... 8.8

Results favoring soft phosphate by 2.19 phosphoric acid over acidulated acid, equivalent to about 5 per cent. available phosphate of lime.

FERTILIZING IN OLDEN TIMES—SEVENTY YEARS EXPERIENCE WITH MARL PHOSPHATE.

"Father's farm was a deep yellow clay. The timber was chestnut' oak, hickory, etc. It had been rented until the tenant could not cut any clover or timothy for hay; no wheat, and but a few bushels of corn, oats and rye. At the first, father and the neighbors began to look around for a fertilizer, for they had but a small quantity of stable manure; this was spread very sparingly on a few acres of land near the barn to raise a few bushels of wheat, corn and oats, and a few loads of hay, and he said it was a few, just a few, for a 160-acre farm to produce.

JERSEY SAND.

"When I got to be about seven years of age, he and his neighbors got to hauling ashes from Philadelphia, thirty miles away. It was brought up in sloops to the nearest landing—Bordentown, on the Delaware river—then he and ten to fifteen of his neighbors would go with their teams and haul it to one of their farms. These ashes only just about paid expenses, with a small margin in favor of the farmer. After a few years this source of getting a fertilizer came to an end by the introduction of anthracite coal; and now the farmers were in a quandary and the question was often asked, 'What can we get for a fertilizer?' For there was not a pound of any kind manufactured that the writer ever heard of; but they were soon relieved of their perplexity—a substance was found in the ground, and right under some of their poor farms, which subsequently proved to be one of the best fertilizers. All that some farmers had to do was to uncap a pit and dig it out. This fertilizer was called 'marl.' Father and his neighbors had to haul it about five miles, and the writer well remembers the many cold mornings and blustering, stormy days, and how he and his brother had to be up by 5 o'clock, feed the stock, swill the swine, harness and hitch up, and off to the 'Pemberton Marl Pits,' chop out the frozen lumps, load up, drive five miles home to the field, spread it out, feed and back again for the second load—two loads a day. This marl cost us twenty five cents a load at the pit.

JERSEY MARL.

"Marl soon became in great demand all over the State, and many a worthless acre was made productive. After using marl several years, to the great benefit of the farmer, it was suggested that lime would be quite an acquisition, as there was not a particle of lime in the soil. All the lime we used had to be shipped from the kilns, over in Pennsylvania, to within seven or eight miles of our farm. It was in large lumps, was hauled and thrown in heaps; water was hauled and thrown on to slack it, then hauled and spread over the field at the rate of from twenty-five to fifty bushels to the acre. On real poor land we dare not put on over twenty to twenty-five bushels to the acre, but when we had a large quantity of coarse manure or a good grass sod to plow under with it, we could put on fifty bushels to the acre, and as the soil became richer in vegetation, etc., could put on more manure; then we increased the number of bushels of lime to sixty or more to the acre.

"There is not any fertilizing quality in

LIME

of itself, yet it has the peculiar power to hasten the decomposition of vegetable matter, and so make it available as plant food. Lime will also correct the acidity in soil.

"Our Jersey marl proved to be a grand fertilizer, and we found that lime judiciously used was really an acquisition, and after years of lugging and tugging, for it was very laborious work for team and teamster, and a tremendous wear and tear on wagons and harness, we had the satisfaction of seeing our barns, cribs and cellars well filled with hay, grain, vegetables, etc.

"Really like that 'certain rich man' we read of in an old book, 'whose ground brought forth so plentifully he had not room to bestow his fruits, so he thought within himself, this will I do: I will pull down my barns and build greater,' and thus did my father, and when I left the old domicile and grange in 1844 for Ohio, he had built and rebuilt until he had sufficient 'room to bestow his fruits,' and his neighbors did likewise, for about all the farmers in those counties became prosperous farmers, the result of marl and lime, industry, frugality and economy; and there are many farms in Ohio, Indiana and other States in the Mississippi Valley, notorious for its fertility, that could be made to produce double, and sometimes treble, by a judicious use of marl and lime."—G. W. Emley, in Agricultural Economist.

MARL AND SOFT PHOSPHATE.

The marl of New Jersey differs but little from the soft phosphate of Florida, especially the Welshton deposits. The New Jersey marl, however, contains only 9 per cent. phosphate of lime, while the Florida marl contains, on an average, 54 per cent., besides 20 per cent. lime, 4 per cent. magnesia, 8 per cent. iron and aluminum, soda, etc., making it five times more valuable than that of New Jersey. Hundreds of tests in Florida and adjoining States on fields and orange groves attest the great value of Florida marl phosphate as a fertilizer.

FLORIDA'S NATURAL MANURIAL RESOURCES.

Florida has unlimited quantities of marl phosphate, muck (more valuable than stable manure) and scrub oak with which to make ashes (the cheapest form of potash), which, in combination with stable manure, makes a complete fertilizer for grove, field or garden. Florida should be the garden spot of the world.

The approved formula per acre is for average Florida soil:

Prepared Soft Phosphate, 500 lbs $2.00
Stable Manure, dry, 1,000 lbs 1 00
Hard wood Ashes, home-made, 500 lbs........................... 3.00

$6.00—Less transportation

This should be well mixed before spreading. In the absence of stable manure substitute dry and thoroughly pulverized muck.

Poor pine land needs humus, and will be greatly benefited by spreading muck upon the surface.

For vegetables, or other products that draw heavily from the soil, the above formula shouln be increased, possibly doubled.

KAOLIN AND GYPSUM.

Among the important discoveries of mineral wealth growing out of the search for phosphate none are of greater value than kaolin.

In 1770, Josiah Wedgworth (father of the famous ware that bears his name) said: "Florida kaolin is of great purity, and very valuable in fine carved work." Florida kaolin was used centuries ago, but for want of transportation facilities was for a time, like the treasures of Pompeii and Rome, buried in oblivion.

The report of the United States geological survey, 1891, speaking of Florida kaolin, says:

"The recent discovery of sedimentary kaolin in the miocene formation of the State bids fair to be one of the most important events in the history of the China clay industry." Tested at the national manufactory at Sevris, it proved fully equal to the famous kaolin of Limoges.

Cornwall kaolin contains 46.27 silica; that of Florida, 46.11. Alumina should be about 40; of this the kaolin of Limoges has 42, Chinese, 33.70, Florida, 39.55.

The large kaolin deposits are principally confined to Lake county. Kaolin rests on eocene limestone and is from twenty-five to thirty feet in thickness. In places it outcrops, but mostly has an overburden of two or more feet of ferruginous sand. Estimating the average depth of the crude kaolin at twenty-five feet and the per cent. of prepared clay ready for shipment at 33 per cent., it will give 12,000 tons to the acre.

The principal company now operating is the Standard Kaolin Co., with headquarters in Ocala, Fla.

GYPSUM.

Among the many recent important discoveries in Florida is gypsum. This material, generally found in volcanic regions, belongs to the Mesozoic or Secondary age. Gypsum is found in Virginia, Tennessee, Michigan and Kentucky, but not till 1889 was it known in Florida.*

The most celebrated gypsum beds in the world are those of Monmartre, near Paris. These quarries are classical ground, having furnished Cuvier the material upon which he based his philosophic history of life on the earth.

Gypsum is a mineral, the natural bihydrated calcium sulphate, and is extensively used as a fertilizer; also in the manufacture of glass, porcelain, etc., and in many of the arts.

---
*Colonel Adam Eichleberger was the first to discover gypsum in Florida, on his orange grove on the Withlacoochee river, where there are large deposits.

THE BLUE AND THE GRAY.

ONE PEOPLE, ONE COUNTRY, ONE FLAG, ONE DESTINY!

OCALA, Dec. 16, 1891.—Forty or fifty Confederate veterans met here in the opera house this evening, representing Pensacola, Monticello, Jacksonville, Dade City, Brooksville, Orlando, Sanford and other places.

On motion, Capt. J. B. Johnston was called to the chair, and Wm. Fox was made secretary. Subsequently they were made permanent chairman and secretary.

Capt. Johnston's remarks on taking the chair were eloquent and full of pathos. Though taken by surprise he was so full of the subject that a month's preparation could not have improved his remarks.

As the veterans filled into the hall Mrs. E. W. Agnew, Mrs. Col. Badger, Mrs. Gen. Dickinson, Mrs. Dozier, Mrs. S. W. Cary, Mrs. Gen. Finley, Mrs. Bullock, Mrs. John Dunn, Mrs. C. J. Allerd and a number of pretty young ladies and little girls pinned a lovely rose on the lappel of each coat. The ladies named, in honor of their heroic service during the war, were afterward invited to seats on the stage.

At 8 o'clock Capt. Johnston called the delegates again to order. On motion of Col. J. M. Martin, Capt. J. H. Welsh, of the Grand Army of the Republic, who was present by special invitation, and Dr. Dwelly, also a Grand Army of the Republic man, were invited to seats by the side of the chairman. Capt. Welsh made a most eloquent and amusing speech, which set the audience in roars of laughter, followed by sympathy at the more pathetic periods.

Col. H. W. Lord moved that a committee of four, the chairman, the major-general, Dr. Wallace of Dade City, and Capt. Merrin of the Plant City Courier, be appointed to draft a constitution and by-laws to govern the State organization of Confederate Veterans.

After speeches by Dr. Dwelly, Col. Long, Col. Cooper, Dr. Maxwell and others, Col. Byrd moved a hand-shake all round between the "Rebs" and "Yanks" who were present, which ceremony was performed amid much merriment and good feeling. Col. Cooper's remarks were sublimely eloquent and patriotic and brought tears to every eye in the audience.

The proceedings and resolution of the ex-Confederate Camp at Monticello, Fla., were read. They are as follows:

Before the Camp proceeded to regular business, at 2 p. m., and soon after recalling the Camp to attention, Commander W. Capers Bird said:

COMRADES: We recognize the fact that the war is over. The South fought for a separate government, not in enmity to our brothers of the North, but for what we, at the time, thought to be the safety and stability of our social and political institutions. But the God of Battles has settled the issue, and we bow honestly and candidly to the result. Hereafter we shall have one people, one flag, one destiny, one country. The North fought for the Union and won. We hail the old Federal soldiers as brothers, as men who were worthy our steel in the hour of battle. I regret that some of those who wore the blue are not with us to-day in a re-union which would testify our appreciation of their valor and generosity, and of the fact that we are once more an indissoluble Union of indestructible States.—Florida Standard.

WHICH WAS UNANIMOUSLY APPROVED.

Adjutant Wright, at the conclusion of Colonel Bird's remarks, moved that a vote of approval or disapproval be taken at once. On this motion, put to the house by Major Simpkins, there was a unanimous voice of approbation, showing that the ex-Confederate soldiers, while faithful to the memories of the past and quick to resent any imputation upon the patriotism and honor of their dead comrades or themselves, stood ready to defend the Union, the Constitution and the enforcement of the laws for the future.

The letter of Capt. John H. Welsh, department commander department of Florida, G. A. R., in acknowledgment of a communication from Col. Bird endorsing action of ex-Confederate camp, Monticello, Fla., as follows, was also read:

WELSHTON, FLA., Dec. 10, 1891.

Colonel W. Capers Bird:

DEAR SIR: After reading your elegant address to the Confederate Camp of Monticello, which you have the honor to command, I said Solomon himself was not wiser, nor was not Cicero when pleading with his countrymen for unity more eloquently patriotic.

Thirteen years ago, after spending a winter in the South, I said "the soldier of the South is to-day loyal, and should the old flag become endangered, he would be found fighting as gallantly in its defense as he ever fought for the Confederacy." I have since seen no reason to change the views then expressed. Lee said at Appomattox: "The war is over." The South will keep the covenant. An accasional young orator of the day (God bless her) to the contrary notwithstanding.

Your declaration "henceforth we shall have one people, one flag, one destiny, one country," unanimously endorsed by your camp, dispels the mist and rain of a quarter of a century.

"From our dead foemen comes no chiding forth,
We live a peace. Heaven has no South, no North,
With roots of tree and flower and fern and heather,
God reaches down and clasps our hands together."

Kindly convey to your camp the best wishes of a Union soldier, whose fondest desire is a perfect union, and believe me to be sincerely your friend.

JOHN H. WELSH.

The resolution was unanimously adopted. The resolution and letter of Capt. Welsh were ordered spread upon the minutes and read in every camp.—From the *Florida Standard.*

THE G. A. R. OF FLORIDA AT DETROIT—THEY ARE ACCOMPANIED BY THE "GRAYS."

THE LAND OF FLOWERS GREETS THE CITY OF STRAITS—A SUPERB BOUQUET PRESENTED BY THE G. A. R. VETERANS.

From the Detroit Sunday News, Aug 9, 1892.

The car load of orange trees, palms, ferns and other products of Florida which the Grand Army veterans from the "Land of Flowers" brought to Detroit were yesterday formally presented to the city by Dept. Commander John H. Welsh. The presentation speech was made in the mayor's office in the presence of an audience of representative citizens. Others of the Florida delegation present were Asst. Adjt. Gen. W. J. Allen, A W. Gates, Col. Hizzard, C. F. Avery, Col. Geo. F. Foote, a retired army officer, and Cash Thomas, superintendent of the Florida Semi Tropical Exposition. Commander Welsh made a happy presentation speech. He said:

"The trans-Atlantic garden of the Hesperides sends greeting to the metropolis of the "Old Lake State," tne home of a future president, and bids me present you this little token—a few samples of our products.

"But I have another and higher mission. It is said that Michigan has enough pine to build a fence seventy five feet high around the Western continent, and conjecture places operations at not later than 1892. We know something of 'Wolverines' and the absence of the word fail in their vocabulary, should steam, however, get crosswise in the 'biler.' I am here to say a word for Florida, draw on us to any extent for pine and crackers."*

"Returning, like the prodigal son, after thirty years' absence, brings to mind an incident of my first visit to Detroit thirty-five years

---
*Native Floridians. 5W

ago. A woman dying of consumption, penniless and alone, seeking the home of her childhood on the opposite shore, whom it was my privilege to aid. A night or two later she came to me in white robes and said, 'Life's fitful fever is over; I reached home only to die, and am now in heaven.' It was only a dream, no doubt, but from that day to this, whether in the peaceful walks of life or in the din of battle, the gem city, nestling between the 'great lakes,' has been associated in my mind with angels.

"I might tell you of America's mighty onward march, for the tramp, tramp of old comrades on your streets, teaching the lesson of loyalty, recalls many memories of stockades and Indian wars in Detroit, when you were the advanced post in the march of the western empire, or of the wonderful growth of your city since last I saw it; but I take for granted you prefer hearing something of the wonderland of America, the new home of my adoption, for though you are on the confines of the British dominions and we on the Gulf of Mexico, our interests are mutual, our prosperity identical."

"No pent-up Utica contracts our powers,
For the whole bondless continent is ours."

"Florida might well be compared to the depreciated securities of the millionaire—locked up for a time as worthless, suddenly they are quoted, the owner recollects his possessions, they are drawn forth and found to be 'legal tender.' Florida has had to exercise the virtue of patience, a resort for consumptives, home of perpetual summer:

"Where the buds ever blossom, the stars ever shine,
And all save the eight ballot box is divine."

"But the dream is over. New York and London are everywhere. American capital and vim are pushing everything aside in the struggle for the billions in our sandhills, lakes and rivers. The sanitarium of the world, a wilderness of oleanders, orange trees, palmettoes, lemons, pines and magnolias, no longer hiding her unquestioned possibilities under a golden haze, has thrown off the sleep of ages and proudly takes her place among the great States of the Union.

"For the sportsman we have myriads of game, for the antiquarian rich stores of tradition, and for the historian there is always the Spanish city of St. Augustine, old Fort Marion, Matanzas and Fort Pickens, the landing place of De Soto, Ponce de Leon, the battlefields of the French and the Spaniards and the fountain of eternal youth."

"You never know a gentleman until you have stretched your legs under his mahogany. We want you to know us as we are, to see us in our homes—so come to Florida. We will show you lakes, rivers and seacoast teeming with fish, Flagler's $2,000,000 Ponce de Leon, Plant's palace hotel, with its silver domes and its pointed minerets glistening like diamonds in the sun, a modern Venice, with white-winged messengers of commerce and pleasure turned to every point of the globe, Silver Springs and the famous Indian river, railroads equipped with every modern appliance, steamers equal to those upon your picturesque river, newspapers whose pens reach around the globe, treasures that put Solomon's mines to shame, more cigars manufactured in a day than you ever conceived of, a people who dry up and blow away when they want to die, a basket of oranges for every man, woman and child in the United States, thousands of acres of phosphate, the depth of which has not been reached at fifty feet; ships from every commercial nation on the globe at Fernandina, Key West and Pensacola, the Sub-Tropical and Semi-Tropical at Jacksonville and Ocala, respectively, Tallahassee, 'The City of Roses,' sitting like ancient Rome upon her seven hills, and everywhere and always 'Caped mile failte.'"

President Livingston of the park commission, in the absence of Mayor Pingree, who was indisposed by overwork during the encampment, accepted the gift on behalf of the city in a neat speech, in which he said that from an extended visit to Florida last winter he could corroborate all that Commander Welsh had said of her beauties and her resources. He had traveled in many countries, but he had never found any so pleasant as Florida. He could attest that her hospitality and her possibilities are boundless. He had seen trees bearing 3,000 oranges, and a luxuriant crop of pineapples growing on what had been third-rate pine land. He was shown while there a phosphate mine from which $270,000 worth of phosphate had been taken from half an acre.

"The exhibit was taken to Belle Isle yesterday afternoon. It will be displayed at the park exposition and then kept permanently at the park.

"An interesting feature of the National Encampment, and one that created much enthusiasm, was a delegation of the Florida Grays, accompanying the Department of Florida G. A. R."

PUBLIC SCHOOLS IN FLORIDA.

Taking the number of schools, viz: 2.333, and placing the population at 400,000, Florida has a public school for every 170 of her population, old and young, white and negro. Census 1890.

In expenditures for public instruction, white and negroes are treated impartially. The average cost of tuition (cost of buildings not included) is $7.81. School buildings are erected by the patrons.

Number of Schools	2.333
Number of White Schools	1,746
Number of Negro Schools	587
Total Enrollment of White Youth	55,191
Total Enrollment of Negro Youth	37,281
Number of Youth of School Age	113,647
Average Daily Attendance	64,819
Number of White Teachers Employed	1,849
Number of Negro Teachers Employed	661
Average Salary of Teachers per Month	$57 72
Total Expenditures for Schools	$516,532 70

STATE INSTITUTIONS.

The State institutions of education are the Florida Agricultural and Mechanical College, located at Lake City, Columbia county; the West Florida Seminary, located at Tallahassee; the East Florida Seminary, located at Gainesville; the Institute for the Blind and Deafmutes, located at St. Augustine; the Normal College for the training of white teachers, located at De Funiak Springs, and the Normal College for the training of negro teachers, located at Tallahassee; tuition in each and all of these is entirely without cost to pupils.

FLORIDA AGRICULTURAL AND MECHANICAL COLLEGE.

This institution is designed not only to give a liberal literary education but to impart also a knowledge of the theory and practice of economcal and successful farming and an industrial training, consisting of tool craft, mechanical drawing, together with special courses in civil engineering, a business course, telegraphy and type-writing, at the option of the student or his parents. An excellent faculty has been placed in charge, large and commodious college buildings and dormitories are supplied and equipped in each of their special departments and supplied with scientific apparatus and appliances, and is now ready for the literary, agricultural and mechanical education of the young men of the State. The expense of living at the college has been reduced to the minimum, being at a cost of $9.00 per month. Wholesome, substantial food is supplied. Students are offered an opportunity to reduce this by working on the farm and college grounds at an allowance per hour.

ANCIENT, COLONIAL AND MODERN.   67

This school is, by the law creating it, one in which military tactics and science must be taught, and is under military discipline and system. This, though an excellent feature of a sound education, is by no means paramount, but subordinate, and supplements the main features of the college work. It is a feature, however, admirable, in that it begets a manliness of deportment and carriage, courage and thorough system.

Taking the average of new schools and expenditures, the number of schools at the present time, December, 1893, would be 2,419; the number of scholars 116,986, and the yearly expenditures $638,139.80.

FLORIDA POLITICS.

Florida may be said to be nothing if not political—a condition prevalent in the South. Just now there are three parties.

The several platforms may be summarized as follows:

DEMOCRATIC ISSUES.

1. Economy in public expenditure.
2. Tariff for revenue only.
3. No force bill.

REPUBLICAN ISSUES.

1. Protection to American industries.
2. A sound and staple currency.
3. A fair and free ballot.

PEOPLE'S PARTY ISSUES.

1. Free and unlimited coinage of gold and silver.
2. Increased circulating medium loaned by the Government at 2 per cent. per annum.
3. Government ownership and control of modes of transmission and transportation.

Of the Democratic issues, the first is disposed of by the fact that the present Democratic Congress was practically as extravagant as the preceding Republican Congress; while the third (the force bill) loses much of its importance in the curious fact that it has never been adopted as a party measure, and was voted down by a Republican Congress, leaving but a single issue, as follows:

We denounce the Republican protective tariff as a fraud upon the labor of the great majority of the American people for the benefit of a few. We declare it to be a fundamental principle of the Democratic party that the Federal Government has not the constitutional power to enforce and collect tariff duties, except for the purpose of revenue only.

Of the issues of the Republican party, the second is but a reiteraion, the currency and coinage of silver having ceased to be party ssues; while the third, in the form of the so-called force bill, having been rejected by a Republican Congress, scarcely deserves the dignity of a place in the party platform, leaving but protection to American industries.

The Republican party stands upon the following plank:

We demand that the imposition of duties on foreign imports shall be made not for revenue only, but that in raising the required revenues for the Government such duties shall be so levied as to afford security in our diversified industries, and protection to the rights and usages of the laborer, to the end that active and intelligent labor, as well as capital, may have its just reward, and the laboring man his full share in the National prosperity.

Of the principles of the People's party but the third can be classed as National, the second being little more than a monetary transaction benefiting the few; while the first is founded on false estimates of value or personal gain. The American silver dollar, not possessing the intrinsic value it represents, leaving, as in the case of the other parties, but the following important plank:

Transportation being a means of exchange and a public necessity, the Government should own and operate the railroads in the interest of the people.

The telegraph and telephone, like the postoffice system, being a necessity for the transmission of news, should be owned and operated in the interest of the people.

The Transportation Lines of Florida.

The history of Florida could not be written without taking into account the transportation lines of the State, for to them Florida is almost wholly indebted for the marvelous prosperity of the past decade.

In 1881 there were three railroads in Florida; the J., P. & M., from Jacksonville to Chattahoochee. The Transit, from Fernandina to Cedar Keys, and a short line from St. Marks to Tallahassee. Throughout the balance of the State, except on the St. Johns and Ocklawaha rivers, silence reigned, for only the crack of the cowboy's lash broke the everlasting stillness.

Ancient as is Florida and wonderful as are her natural resources, a dozen years ago she possessed but a dismantled fort or two; a limited and listless population; herds of cattle; the remnant of a brave but merciless race of "red-skins;" fish, alligators and an occasional consumptive Yankee.

The actual necessities of life were easily obtained, and it was the boast of the Floridian that he was never in a hurry; nor was there need to be, for there were no means of transportation, except on the line of navigable rivers, and whatever he produced beyond his necessities was a waste of material. There were no markets except for cattle, which could be moved on foot; so the sun shone and the indolent slumbered. But the unexpected occurred; the screech of the locomotive was heard throughout the land, and Florida awoke to an undreamed era of prosperity. Enterprise, backed by capital, saw the possibilities of the State; railroads stretched out in every direction. Every hamlet is now in touch with the marts of the world. Hundreds of cities have sprung into being out of the desert places. Land in many parts of the State has increased in value a hundred fold. The product of the grove and farm is but three days from New York or Boston. Palatial hotels, some of them costing millions of dollars, are everywhere, and 50,000 tourists winter in Florida—a condition of things impossible without transportation.

Florida is now said to be fifth in railroad construction and third in train mileage among the States of the Union, but in increase of mileage according to population there is no comparison, Florida outstripping them all. Three of these magnificent roads are nearly parallel lines, tapping South America at Gulf ports, and having direct connections North, East and West, practically annihilating both time and space—Tampa being but forty hours from New York or Chicago.

The surprising feature of Florida railroad construction, however, is the vast network of lateral roads in every direction.

The transportation lines of Florida cost the enormous sum of $75,000,000; employ 7,000 people, and expend annually more than $6,500,000 in the State.

Following the railways in order of importance are the steamship and river lines, which yearly put in circulation $1,000,000.

The following are some of the most important lines of transportation:

The Tropical Trunk Line--The J., T. & K. W. System.

Tapping the great arteries of trade and travel, North and West, at Jacksonville, the metropolis of Florida, this popular system of railways and inland steamers connects Lake Worth, the paradise of the East Coast, Punta Gorda, the extreme southern limit of inland traffic, and Tampa, the modern Venice on the Gulf of Mexico, with a long arm from Palatka, through the interior, touching Gainesville, Ocala, Leesburg, Pemberton and other points of commercial importance.

Taking the "vestibuled" fast mail south, we stop at Orange Park, a pretty little hamlet, embowered in mammoth oaks. Next at Magnolia, a fashionable winter resort, consisting of a palatial hotel and pretentious cottages. Ten minutes later we are at Green Cove Springs, noted for its sulphur baths, comfortable hotels, romantic "Lovers' Lane," and handsome residences; and an hour later pull up at Palatka, where connections are made with the Florida Southern, Georgia Southern and Florida, Daytona, St. Augustine and all points on the St. Johns and Ocklawaha rivers, via daily line of steamers. Palatka boasts gas works, street railway, water works, fine hotels (the Putnam House is among the finest and largest in the State), beautiful scenery and a boundless hospitality.

Leaving Palatka, our first halt is at Seville, one of the many pretty "railroad towns" of the State. Shortly after we are at Enterprise, and while yet it is day, pull into Titusville, the *Key City* of the east coast, familiarly known as the Indian River country, of which the poet sings:

>Palm, palmetto, lime and cypress,
>And the wind-swept cedar trees,
>Live oaks draped with mist-like mosses,
>Grace my banks; yea, more than these.
>Fruits, whose life is tropic sunshine; flowers,
>With brilliance rich and rare,
>And when stars shine on my waters
>There is fragrance everywhere.

The roadway from Jacksonville is lined with thriving towns, endless groves and cozy cottages—a delightfully rural panorama not soon to be forgotten.

Titusville is a thriving town of 2,50 population, and is noted for its beautiful vegetable farms and oranger goves. It is the county seat of Brevard County. The famous Turnbull "Hammock" begins on the northern edge of the town, and extends for a distance of forty miles, an unbroken body of most fertile soil.

A glance at Titusville, and we are off via the Jacksonville, Tampa and Key West line of Steamers for Rockledge—the picturesque! Here one might linger in the lap of summer, counting only the years—possibly the *hotel bills,* but there are said to be even greater attractions, so we push on to Jupiter, the southern limit of river navigation, where we take the Jupiter & Lake Worth Railway—a part of this system—for Juno, and thence via steamer for Pitts' Island, Oak Lawn, Riveria, Palm Beach, etc., tourist resorts on Lake Worth.

Beautiful Lake Worth! home of summer breezes and endless sunshine. What pen can tell thy charms, what brush can do thee justice? Nature, with omnipotent hand, and *man,* with the magic power of gold, have conspired to make thee exquisite! Nature was bountiful—man was lavish. Incomparable blending of Art and Nature—thou art, indeed, a *bower* of *enchantment!*

The officers of this system are:

Major J. H. Durkee, Receiver, Jacksonville, Fla.
W. B. Coffin, General Manager, Jacksonville, Fla.
G. D. Ackerly, General Passenger Agent, Jacksonville, Fla.
James Menzies, General Freight Agent, Jacksonville, Fla.

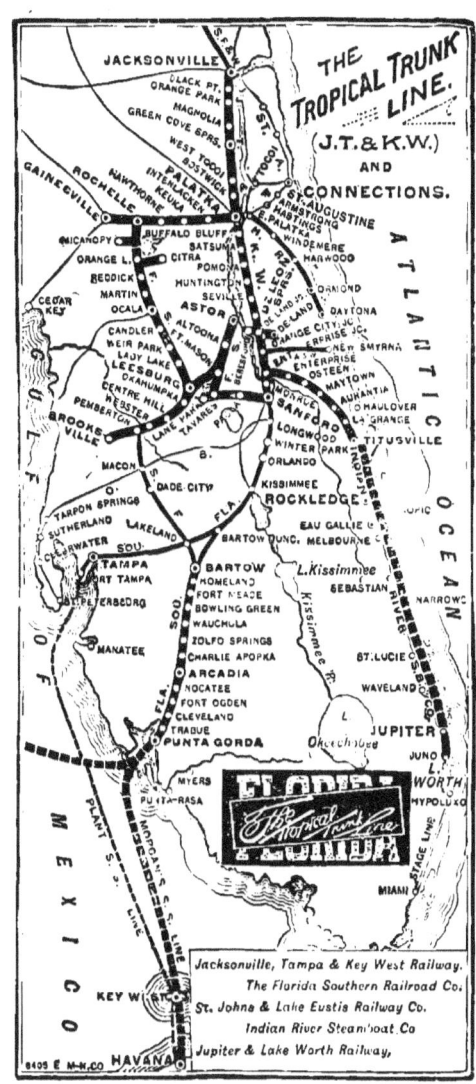

A Typical Piny Woods Lake. Fla. Sou. Ry.

A Thoroughfare of the Tropics—The Florida Southern Railway.

(Now a Part of the J., T. & K. W. System.)

The Florida Southern Railroad, beginning at Palatka, the head of deep navigation on the St. Johns, where it connects with the main line of the system to which it belongs, was commenced in 1881, and before the close of the season the line was in operation to Gainesville. In 1882 the southern extension was begun and the road completed to Ocala—the "Brick City"—which, before the building of the road, was but a jumble of cabins.

Early in the spring of '83, Major Conant, a man of great executive ability, was made General Manager. Work-shops were enlarged and fitted with modern machinery. A foundry was built, skilled workmen employed and cars and locomotives constructed. "On to Leesburg" was the order, and during 1883 forty miles of track were laid. The following year the road was extended to Brooksville, and a year or two later was further extended to Punta Gorda, its present terminus, where it connects by steamship with New Orleans, New York, Europe and important points in South America.

The branches of the Florida Southern are as follows: Micanopy Junction to Tacoma via Micanopy, and Oaklawn to Citra.

Some idea of the material interests to the State, involved in the construction of this road, may be gathered from the fact that its annual haul of phosphate is over 100,000 tons, and of oranges more than 1,000,000 boxes; besides nearly one-third of all the vegetables raised in the State; and that since its construction, 100 towns and cities have sprung into being on the line of its march. The line—from Palatka to Charlotte Harbor on the Gulf—is, including branches, 375 miles in length.

Punta Gorda—the Naples of America—has a harbor in which the fleets of the world could ride in safety. This is the rendezvous of the yachtsmen, who yearly congregate in Charlotte Harbor to revel in sunshine, tropical scenery and tarpon fishing. The bay is thirty miles long and connects by lines of steamers with St. James—a popular winter resort—Punta Rassa and Fort Myers on the Caloosahatchee. Punta Gorda possesses one of the finest hotels in the State, with accommodations for four hundred guests, built by the Florida Commercial Company.

The Florida Southern passes through some of the best lands in the State, and the scenery is varied and beautiful. It pierces the hammocks, rushes through the pines, dashes along the lake shores, and winds and weaves around orange groves, delightful gardens and extensive plantations. The panorama of the route is momentarily changing. It is in turn wild, picturesque and romantic.

This important natural highway to the tropics through the backbone of the State, one of the most progressive and deservedly popular railways of the South, will be changed from a narrow to a broad guage during the summer of 1895, equipped with rolling stock of the latest and most approved designs, and every appliance ingenuity can devise looking to safety and comfort.

The officers of the road are:
F. Q. Brown, President.
R. J. Edwards, Treasurer, Boston.
Capt. W. B. Denham, General Superintendent, Palatka, Fla.

The Tropical Trunk Line comprises the Jacksonville, Tampa & Key West Railway, the Florida Southern Railroad, the Indian River Steamboat Company, the Jupiter & Lake Worth Rail-way, and other separately operated lines.

The Plant System.

There are in the great sub-divisions of labor—mechanics, trade and commerce, men who, by force of intellect, power of combination and extraordinary courage, are distinguished. Men whose ambition it is to overcome the seemingly insurmountable. Men who, disregarding the trammels of precedent, or possible previous failures, boldly advance and conquer. Of such is the man Henry B. Plant, whose life's work forms the text of this article.

To geographically describe the Plant System of railways, ocean and river steamers, would require space beyond the limit we can assign it. Let us, however, imagine a line from Charleston, South Carolina, southward, to Savannah, Brunswick and Jacksonville on the Atlantic; Albany, Thomasville and Montgomery in the west; Sanford, the Everglades, Bartow, Phosphoria and Tampa in South Florida; Mobile, Appalachicola, Homosassa, Port Tampa and Key West on the Gulf of Mexico, and Havana, in the Island of Cuba, the main arm extending north and south through Central Florida, with various branches, and we have some idea of its extraordinary scope.

The following lines of railways and steamers comprise the system:

Railway lines, mileage. Savannah, Florida & Western Railway, 562; Charleston & Savannah Railway, 133; South Florida division of Savannah, Florida & Western Railway, 327; Brunswick & Western Railroad, 171; Alabama Midland Railway, 235; Silver Springs, Ocala & Gulf Railway, 66. Total, 1,494.

Peoples' Line steamers, mileage, Chattahoochee River, 223; Flint River, 36; Appalachicola River, 137. Total, 396.

Plant Steamship Line, mileage, Port Tampa, Key West & Havana Line, 360; Port Tampa & Mobile Line, 360; Port Tampa & Manatee River Line, 36; Port Tampa to Caloosahatchee River, 125; Port Tampa to St. Petersburg, 6. Total, 887.

Recapitulation, mileage—Railway lines, 1,494; steamer lines, 1,283. Total, 2,777.

Studying the maps of to-day, the magnitude of this aggregation of lines of travel and traffic is forced upon us. Not a foot of which existed south of the 31st parallel a dozen years ago. It is not its immensity, however, but its perfection that is astonishing. Roadbeds, cars and steamers being of the most approved construction. Enhanced by numerous and costly hotels, notably the Seminole, at Winter Park, the Tampa Bay Hotel, Tampa, a structure which in extent, elegance and management is the admiration of all beholders, and the Port Tampa Inn and beautiful Queen Anne cottages, built upon piles over the waters of Tampa Bay—the Venice of the Western world.

ALONG THE S. S., O. & G., A BRANCH OF THE PLANT SYSTEM.

Desiring a more thorough knowledge of that almost *terra incognito* along the line of the mysterious S. S., O. & G. Railway—mysterious, however, only because of its devious windings and seemingly endless branches, the writer recently accepted a cordial invitation from General Superintendent O. G. Finch to see the sights, and in the early morning found a special train awaiting the party. Eight a. m. is the time for departure. The mail train is waiting for us to pull out. The conductor nods, a bell rings, and we are started on one of the most interesting trips in this curious land of pleasant surprises.

The general conformation of the S. S., O. & G. might well be likened to an exceedingly crooked Y, with Ocala at the bottom, Inverness at the left-hand upper corner, 43 miles distant, and Hommossa at the extremity of the right extension resting on the Gulf, 50 miles away. This and thirteen of the crookedest branches in existence and you have some idea of this famous railroad.

Dunnellon, named in honor of Florida's lamented son, Hon. John F. Dunn, 25 miles from Ocala, is our first stopping place. This town is the mother of the Florida phosphate industry, some idea of which may be gathered from the fact that in 1892 the shipments were 87,248 gross tons, with a guaranteed analysis of 75 per cent., comprehending an expenditure of $5,000,000 for lands, and an annual expenditure of $400,000 for labor, etc. But a stone's throw from the depot is Dunn's bluff, an almost perpendicular bank of the Withlacoochee, across which the eye is gladdened by one of the most romantic sights on the continent, for here it is that the legendary Wekiva, meandering slowly through green valleys and over-hanging foliage, finally mingles its ever-changing waters with the less beautiful but more practical Withlacoochee.

> "Close beside the meeting waters,
> Long I stood as in a dream,
> Watching how the little river
> Fell into the broader stream.
>
> "Calm and still the mingled current
> Glided to the waiting sea,
> On its breast serenely pictured
> Floating cloud and skirting tree."

Of this spot Moore might well have dreamed when composing that most exquisite of songs—

> "There is not in this wide world
> A valley so sweet
> As the vale on whose bosom
> The bright waters meet."

One of the Plant Line of Ocean Steamers.

We could have lingered here indefinitely, but "all aboard" is heard and three minutes later we are dashing over the Withlacoochee, without a trace of the beautiful little Wekiva. Thirty minutes later we are skirting the famous Tsala Apopka, and at ten o'clock pull up at Inverness, where the S. S., O. & G. connects with the main line of the system.

Inverness, like Dunnellon, is the outgrowth of phosphate development, and although but a little more than two years old, is a place of considerable importance, giving promise of rapid and enduring prosperity. The time alloted is up, good-byes are regretfully said and we are doing a forty mile gate for Citronelle, on the right hand stem of the Y, better known as the branch.

The next place of importance is Crystal River, one of the old landmarks of the Gulf country, famous for its fish, game and oysters, and twenty minutes later we pull up at Homosassa, the Mecca of the sportsman.

Homosassa is a town peculiar unto itself, for nature—not man—is the architect. This sylvan retreat, nestling among tropical foliage, is happily situated, being easy of access to the sea, yet sufficiently distant to obviate the baneful influence to invalids, especially consumptives, of a too close proximity to the gales peculiar to the Gulf. Here the timid, the weary, or the searchers after health may exclaim:

"In quiet bays the storm unspent,
I moor my boat with calm content."

Officials of the Plant System: General officers—H. B. Plant, President; M. F. Plant, Assistant to President; D. F. Jack, Assistant to President; H. S. Haines, Vice President; W. B, McKee, Assistant to Vice-President; R. G. Erwin, Vice-President and General Counsel, 12 West Twenty-third Street, New York; C. D. Owens, Freight Traffic Manager, Savannah, Ga.; B. W. Wrenn, Passenger Traffic Manager, Savannah, Ga.; W. M. Davidson, General Passenger Agent, Jacksonville, Fla.; G. Deming, Traveling Passenger Agent.

J. A. Larnard, Superintendent S. S.. O. & G. Railway, Ocala.

The Florida Central and Peninsular Railroad.

FLORIDA'S GREAT RAILROAD SYSTEM.

There is probably no State in the Union which has in proportion to its population so many miles of railway as Florida. With a population of about four hundred thousand people, of which nearly one-half are of the colored race, it has over 3,000 miles of railway in operation, most of which are broad guage and first class.

At the head of the railway systems in Florida stands confessedly the Florida Central and Peninsular Road, now extending from Columbia, S. C., to Tampa Bay, Cedar Keys, Oviedo, Fernandina, Jacksonville, St. Marks, Tallahassee and River Junction—a total mileage of about one thousand miles.

The man who originated and made possible these great railway systems in Florida was the Hon. David L. Yulee.

Mr. Yulee entered public life as a member of the Legislature in Territorial times; was elected a Delegate in Congress about 1841; secured the admission of Florida as a State in 1845; was elected a Representative in Congress; and before taking his seat elected to the United States Senate, where he remained for many years until the civil war, when he resigned his seat.

With remarkable quickness of apprehension he united great power of accomplishment. Almost immediately after the admission of the State he entertained the idea of effecting the construction of a railway across the peninsula of Florida. After some previous failures he procured a charter in January, 1849, with Isaac Newton, Alfred G. Benson, John Howard, and their associates, by the name of the Atlantic and Gulf Railroad Company, to construct a road between the Atlantic Ocean and the Gulf of Mexico. This charter was awarded in 1854, and George Law became the principal party in the enterprise. These gentlemen were all connected with steamship lines, and anticipated opening a line to the Pacific by steamers to a Florida Atlantic port; thence across the peninsula to the Gulf, with steamship lines to Tehuantepec; thence by rail across that isthmus to the Pacific, connecting with steamship lines to California and South American ports.

The Pacific Railroad was not then built and hardly seriously contemplated, and this project in which Florida was to play so important a part was at once eagerly embraced by Mr. Yulee, and every effort made by him to aid in its accomplishment. At Mr. Law's instance he procured the necessary lands for the Atlantic terminal point. Obtaining lands on the St. Mary's and Fernandina through the agency of the late Joseph Finegan. The road was not built under the George Law charter, it being forfeited by expiration of the limitation of time.

In 1853 Mr. Yulee procured a charter under the name of the Florida Railroad Company, and Mr. Law transferred his terminal interests to parties connected with the new company.

Mr. Yulee was the controlling spirit of the new company, and in order to facilitate the construction of the road united the various interests desiring railroad construction, and procured from the Legislature the passage of an act to encourage a liberal system of internal improvement, which provided for the aid of the State being given to a line, of railroad from Jacksonville to Pensacola and Amelia Island to Tampa Bay, with an extension to Cedar Key, and a canal to connect Lake Harney with Indian River. This aid was to be given in the shape of an indorsement and guarantee by the State of the interest on bonds issued by the railroads to the extent of $10,000 per mile, and also the benefit of any land grants made by the general government. The Florida Railroad was organized, and went to work under the provisions of this act, and received the benefit of this State guarantee and of alternate sections of land within six miles of the line of rail. They also issued what were called Free Land Bonds, based on the security of the land held by the company.

With this aid the Florida Railroad built their road to Cedar Key before 1860, and the railroad from Jacksonville to Lake City and Tallahassee to Lake City were also built, with the further help of town and county bonds.

The civil war came on just as that part of the Florida Railroad from Fernandina to Cedar Key was completed, and of course the property deteriorated during the ensuing four years. For twelve months after the war Mr. Yulee was held as a political prisoner in Fort Pulaski, so that it was not until May, 1866, that he was released and able to assume charge of the road. Twenty-eight miles of the track between Fernandina and Baldwin had been removed; part of it carried to Port Royal by the United States forces, and part of it used to build the road from Live Oak to Lawton by the Confederate forces. The whole equipment in 1866 consisted of but three locomotives, in bad order, two miserable passenger cars, and twenty-one old freight cars.

The Trustees of the Internal Improvement Fund seized the Florida Railroad on account of default in the payment of interest on the guaranteed bonds, and sold the road on November 1, 1866, to E. N. Dickerson, of New York, and the Florida Railroad as a corporation came to an end. The iron rail, however, was of a superior character, having cost $58.50 per ton, and much of it was in use for over thirty years.

After the sale of the road in November, 1866, the name of the road was in 1872 changed to the Atlantic Gulf and West India Transit Railroad Company, and at a later day to Florida Transit Railroad Company. The part of the main line extending from Waldo to Ocala was constructed under the name of the Peninsula Railroad Company, and from Ocala to Wildwood and beyond under the name of the Tropical Florida Railroad. The branch to Leesburg and Tavares under name of Leesburg and Indian River Railroad; Tavares to Orlando as the Tavares and Orlando Railroad; Fernandina to Jacksonville as the Fernandina and Jacksonville Railroad in 1880. In 1883 all these roads, inclusive of the Jacksonville and Lake City and River Junction were merged into one organization under the name of the Florida Railway and Navigation Company. The whole system went into the hands of a receiver, and Col. H. R. Duval was appointed such receiver. At the time this very able and efficient gentleman assumed control of the system it was generally in a very bad condition. Mr. Yulee had some years previously disposed of his interests, being well along in years, the road had become much the worse for wear, and the equipment altogether inefficient.

Col. Duval brought to the work a high reputation as a reorganizer, and with great rapidity proceeded to resuscitate the road, laying down new rails, new cross ties; purchased a large number of new locomotives, coaches and freight cars. Aided by the long experience of the general manager, D. E. Maxwell, Capt. A. O. McDonnell, General Passenger Agent, and others, he soon brought the road into first-class condition. The road was restored to the stockholders, and the name changed to the Florida Central and Peninsular. Col. Duval became the president, and under his control and management it has become one of the largest and best conducted railway systems in the South. Besides building and acquiring a number of extensions and branches in Florida he has purchased the New South Bound Road from Columbia to Savannah, and constructed an entirely new road on the shortest line from Savannah into Florida, connecting with the main line at Yulee for Jacksonville, Tallahassee, Cedar Keys, Tampa and Orlando. Finely equipped luxurious and fast trains now run over all these lines.

Although the Tehuantepec route to the Pacific has never been opened, and consequently Mr. Yulee's expectations of his road forming a link in a great transcontinental line has not yet been realized, it may still happen, as now seems probable that when the Nicarauga Canal is opened, Mr. Yulee's anticipations, so warmly cherished by him forty years since, may become realities in the near future.

Florida owes a debt of gratitude to the memory of Mr. Yulee for the splendid foundations laid for her growth and prosperity, as well also to Col. H. R. Duval, for the maturing and carrying out of the great development and enlargement of the plans of his distinguished predecessors.

There are many points of interest to the lover of nature on the line of the F. C. & P. Railway, notably

SILVER SPRINGS,

the feeder of the Ocklawaha. The "Springs" consist of a cluster of three wells walled with granite, as if by man, from which immense volumes of crystal waters constantly flow. These waters have a silvery tint and are so transparent that at a depth of 60 feet small particles of metal, such as tin, are clearly discernable. The "Springs" are enclosed by a wall of evergreen, shrouded with trailing moss and blossoming vines, all of which are clearly reflected in the eddying waters. To this Spring the following beautiful tribute is paid by Mr. George F. Collom:

> If the scenes where fairies hover
> Are where waters are the clearest,
> With deep skies the b'urst, over,
> And reflected, woodl nds nearest—
> Flashing with a wild bird's wing.
>
> Then must fairies—in the silence
> Underneath a sky dream-haunted,
> Such a sky as fabled islands
> Only, yet have elsewhere vaun'ed—
> Fairies haunt the SILVER SPRING.

Silver Springs might justly be called Nature's mirror. Another, and if possible greater attraction, is the historic

SUWANEE RIVER,

the scene of that inimitably pathetic song "Way Down Upon the Suwanee River." The Suwanee River Spring is unsurpassed as a resort, its colonaded hotel annex and cottages furnished throughout with taste and elegance. Private baths in most all rooms. Hot and cold sulphur water. Grand plunge bath. Most excellent table and perfect service, making it one of the most desirable of homes for the tourist as well as seeker after health.

Looking over the map of the F. C. & P. of to-day, the mind finds it difficult to grasp its wonderful scope, its seemingly impossible magnitude. Let us, however, imagine three lines of steel.

First.—From Columbia, S. C. to Tampa, Florida, via Denmark, Fairfax, Savannah, Yulee, Jacksonville, Baldwin, Waldo, the famed Silver Springs, Ocala, Wildwood, Lacoochee, Dade City, Plant City and Turkey Creek, with branches from Wildwood via Leesburg, Tavares and Apopka, to Sanford on Lake Monroe—the head of navigation on the St. Johns river—Longwood, Lake Jessup, Orlando and Kissimmee on Lake Tohopekaliaga and from Turkey Creek to Alafia.

Second.—From Jacksonville—the metropolis of Florida—to River Junction, on the Chattahoochee River, via Baldwin, Lake City. Ellaville, at which point the road crosses the famed Suwanee, Drifton and Tallahassee—the capital of Florida, with branches. Drifton to Monticello and Tallahassee to St. Marks.

Third—From Fernandina to Cedar Keys (the old Transit Railway—familiarly known as the Yulee Road) via Yulee, Callahan, Baldwin, Hampton, Waldo, Gainesville and Bronson, and we have some conception of this modern leviathan of railway construction. It is not, however, the magnitude of this giant that surprises the beholder, but the perfection of its road-bed, the elegance of its equipment and comprehensive management.

What this Southern Hercules of traffic will next undertake is, at best but conjecture. A line of ocean grey-hounds from Tampa down the coast of Mexico to the Bahamas, Nassau and Jamaica, returning around the capes of Cuba, is however among the possibilities.

The officers of this road are:
H. R. Duval, President.
D. E. Maxwell, General Manager.
T. A. Phillips, Assistant General Manager.
N. S. Pennington, Traffic Manager.
A. O. MacDonell, General Passenger Agent.
W. H. Pleasants, General Freight Agent.
Walter G. Coleman, General Traveling Agent.

The Clyde Line.

While the prosperity and consequent usefulness, of every line of steamers plying upon the waters of Florida, is a matter of general congratulation, the success of the Clyde Line is especially gratifying, for in it we see the morning of a new commercial departure, the dawn of a new era of development.

Seven years ago (1886), Wm. P. Clyde, of the Clyde Line, was approached in New York with the query: "Are you going to run a steamer to Florida? Why, Mr. Clyde, you never can make a steamer pay to Florida; there is no business," to which Mr. Clyde replied, "Well, we can stand it five years. I am going to try it that long; if it don't pay then we can quit."

The first steamer of the line, the Cherokee, reached Jacksonville in November, 1886, with half a cargo and with a passenger list which might almost have been placed among the ciphers.

To-day there are six steamers on the line, the cost of which was over three million dollars, besides the St. Johns river fleet of four steamers. Some idea of the importance to Florida of this steamship company is shown in the fact that their yearly expenditures here are $550 000, the greater part of which is expended in Jacksonville. The employes now number 600.

It might be supposed, starting seven years ago with one steamer, that now when there is one for every day in the week, the limit was reached, but such is not the case, for, though unknown to the public, it is a fact that two additional passenger steamers of the most improved order are in contemplation for this line, the volume of travel and traffic being so great that several of the steamers no longer touch at Charleston, but ply directly between Jacksonville and New York.

An important item of freight over this line, at times taxing its resources, is cotton, from Texas and Louisiana, while the appreciation of the traveling public is demonstrated in the fact that its passenger list is always full, even in the dullest season.

The Florida ships of this line plying between Jacksonville and New York, are the Cherokee, Seminole, Iroquois, Algonquin, Yemassee and Delaware. All the steamships of this line are fitted with every modern appliance of safety and comfort; and that they are ably managed is attested by the fact that not an accident of note has occurred to one of these ships since the inauguration of the line.

The Philadelphia line of the Clyde system are the elegant ships

Delaware, Winyah and Oneida. Weekly between Jacksonville and Philadelphia.

The St. Johns river steamers are the City of Jacksonville, Fred'k deBary, Everglade and Welaka.

The New York docks of this line are the largest in that city, while the business facilities of Jacksonville have doubled in the past year.

No tour of Florida can be said to be complete without "doing" the St. Johns, so we take passage at Jacksonville on the elegant steamer Frederick de Bary of the Clyde River Line, and on a glorious sunshiny day find ourselves gliding over the historic "River of May," as it was known by the French and Spaniards. Many pretty towns and villages are passed, notably Green Cove Springs, and as the shadows of night are falling we are at Palatka, the "Gem City," and take advantage of a short stay to visit points of interest.

NIGHT ON THE ST. JOHNS.

There are many picturesque spots about the "Gem City," but nothing to compare with "Big Bend," or, as it is commonly called "The Hammock," to which our wandering footsteps led. Two steamers, from "up country," racing for the landing, are swinging round "the point," throwing a glare upon the waters and belching fourth volumes of smoke, reaching far astern. Vulcans of the past— shadows of the dread Inferno. A steamer under way is always an interesting study, so we light a cigar, and intent only on watching the race to a finish, are startled with: "Well, you old Republican, how are you any way?" and there stands Capt. Bill K——, the best known man in Florida, for (as he says) There is not a foot of it he has not traversed. Five minutes later the boats are at their wharves, and turning to the Captain, I remark, "This is a scene of enchantment."

"Enchantment," said the Captain, "Why, sir," (Bill always says 'sir' when his usual serenity is disturbed) "there is more enchantment, more romance, if you will, under the shadow of these old oaks than you ever conceived—an indefinable something which not even an Anchorite could resist. Why sir, it was here under these very branches that I——; but what nonsense. You Yankees haven't a thought but of dollars. Want to hear the story, do you? Well, I'm in a sort of reminiscent mood to-night, tho' as a rule, I'm not given to story-telling."

THE STORY.

'Twas just after the *wah*, you see, and having determined to squander some of my patrimony in foreign travel, I returned home one evening turning over in my mind how I should break the matter, when, on reaching the gate, I was greeted with, "Oh, Will! you are just in time to see Laura home." Laura Lee—the only daughter of the old Major, up in the edge of the "young hammock," was then in the first blush of womanhood, tall and willowy, with hair the hue of gold, eyes that expressed every pulsation of the soul, skin of alabaster whiteness, and cheeks that rivaled our own beautiful Southern rose in exquisite coloring, a very vision of purity and innocence, about whom my sisters often joked me, but I knew nothing of love, and, as you know, am naturally diffident.

Well, at last we are on our way, and just as we reached this very tree, I felt her tremble, and in my embarrassment, lead her to a seat, possibly the one on which you are sitting.

'Twas a glorious eve, a scene which only the brush of a Turner could depict. * * * On the right, stretching as far as the eye could penetrate, were residences, discernable thro' waving palms and the golden orange, interspersed with mammoth oaks, canopied with floating zephyrs, weird palmettoes, whose heads reached into the clouds, and magnolias, whose white petals made the senses delirious with fragrance, while along the river ran a border of green like a ring of emeralds, and but a stone's throw, launches, row-boats and yachts, in every variety of coloring and construction, lying placidly at their moorings, or floating gently with the tide. While across the river is "Hart's Point," its dry docks, quaint Ocklawaha steamers and seemingly endless groves of lemons, limes, bananas and oranges are reflected in the shadowy but translucent St. Johns; while on the left Palatka's thousand lights, mingled with myriads of twinkling stars, glimmer on the waters, and ever and anon are heard the note of the guitar or mandolin, the melody of song and the twitter of the nightingale—a medley of scenes and songs of which I can give but a faint conception. * * * * * * * * *

Lost for the time to all but the surroundings, I feel a touch upon my arm, a warm breath upon my cheek. A slender arm steals about me, a golden head rests upon my bosom, and I hear the gentlest of voices murmur: "Will, oh Will, I—I love you." I never knew exactly what happened next; I was conscious only of some mysterious, indefinable influence I could not resist, and clasping her to my throbbing heart, showered kisses upon her upturned face, and plighted eternal constancy."

Whether the story was ended, we know not, for out upon the waters is heard the refrain:

"None can tell how much I loved her,
She was good and kind to me;
But Heaven has claimed her for an angel,
Lovely, dark-eyed Laura Lee."

And we turned silently away, the Captain merely remarking, with the glisten of a tear in his eye as we reached the wharf, I'm now in the "sere and yellow" of life, as the poets say, but never come to Palatka without visiting "The Hammock."

Just above Palatka is San Mateo, the scene of the bloody massacre of the Spanish in 1567, and a little later we are at the world-famed Ocklawaha, down which one of the Hart Line of curious little steamers is twisting and turning with apparent abandon, but surely approaching. Drayton Island, the once seat of a powerful people of the forest, is passed, and squeezing out through the narrows we are in Lake George, a fine body of water, resembling an inland sea. Volusia, another of the old Spanish settlements, is speedily left behind, and we are at Astor, where connection is made with the St. Johns and Lake Eustis Railway. From here on the windings are interminable, a labyrinth of devious ways, shrouded in tropical foliage, looking down complacently upon the most tranquil of rivers.

Southward from Jacksonville this most charming of American waterways gradually narrows, finally terminating in beautiful Lake Monroe, 198 miles from Jacksonville, upon the shores of which are Enterprise and Sanford—two of Florida's most famous winter resorts.

Sanford is the terminus of Clyde's St. Johns River Line, and we bid the historic river a silent *au revoir*, not *adieu*.

The Florida officers of the Clyde Line are Major J. A. Leslie, Superintendent, Jacksonville, Fla.; F. M. Ironmonger, Jr., Florida Passenger Agent, Jacksonville, Fla.; John L. Howard, Florida Freight Agent, Jacksonville, Fla.

The Famed Ocklawaha---Florida's Mystic Stream.

Colonel H. L. Hart, a man destined to play an important part in the development of Florida, was born at Guilford, Vt., May 4th, 1827, reached Palatka July 1, 1855, and a week later made the following announcement:

United States Mail.

Change of Proprietorship

Concord Coaches.   **Stage**   Good Horses, Etc.

PILATKA to TAMPA,

Via Orange Spring, Orange Lake, Ocala, **Camp Izard, Augusta, Melendez,** Pierseville, and **Ft. Taylor.**

Stages leave Pilatka and Tampa, Mondays & Thursdays at 7 (resting at night) A.M., arriving at Tampa and Pilatka (respectively) the following Wednesday and Saturdays; thereby affording Invalids a better opportunity for travelling) connecting at Tampa with the

N. Orleans and Key West Steamers,
and at Pilatka with the Steam-Boats for Savannah & Charleston.

Also: Intersecting this line, is a Stage From Ocala, via Flemington, Micanopy, and Newmansville, to Alligator

EXTRA CARRIAGES & HORSES ON HAND,
at Pilatka, to convay Passengers to Micanopy, Elomington, Silver Springs. &c., &c.

ALL EXPRESS BUSINESS PRomptly ATTENDED TO.

OFFice in PILATKA, AT COL. J. O. DUVAL'S HOTEL.
July, 1855,   **H. L. HART, Proprietor.**

In 1860 Col. Hart conceived the idea of putting a line of steamers upon the Ocklawaha. The first steamer of this line was the James Burt, and during the same year he added the steamer Silver Springs; but the civil war coming on put a temporary stop to the enterprise. The war over, he built in succession the Panasoffkee, Ocklawaha, Okahumka, Osceola and Astatula. In the meantime vigorously prosecuting the work of removing the many obstructions which made navigation not only difficult but extremely hazardous, especially from Silver Springs Run to Lakes Griffin, Eustis, Harris and Denham, at which time but six white families lived in the entire "lake region."

This was an eventful period in the history of the State. The present steamers of the line bear the names of three of those first built, namely, the Okahumka, Astatula aud Osceola, a daily line plying between Palatka and Silver Springs, 135 miles. One of the most popular routes on the American continent.

Adapting to the Ocklawaha Byron's famous apostrophe, the quotation would read:

"Nature formed but one such scene and broke the die."

It was of this river that General Grant remarked after his tour of the world: "This is the greatest wonder I have seen." He might have added, "Egypt has her pyramids, Epheseus her Temple of Diana, Babylon her Hanging Gardens, Alexandria the tomb of the Pharos, Olympus her palace of Zeno, Greece the ruins of the Colossus of Rhodes, America the Ocklawaha—the grandest of all; for it is the unapproachable work of the Omnipotent."

Seeing Florida without the Ocklawaha would be as Hamlet without the ghost. So following in the wake of the throng we take passage at Palatka, one of the famed tourist resorts of this almost perpetual summerland, via Hart's Line of Ocklawaha steamers, and on a beautiful mid-winter afternoon are plowing the upper St. Johns on the Steamer Astatula, Capt. C. H. Howard, a sort of infantile Noah's ark, especially constructed for this route, but possessing all the comforts and many of the elegancies of more pretentious construction.

Innumerable groves of the lemon, lime and orange are passed, and as the orb of day is settling below the distant horizon we are at the mouth of the picturesque but seemingly impenetrable Ocklawaha, having accomplished the distance from Palatka, twenty-five miles, in a little more than three hours.

Ascending this most tortuous and (at night) most uncanny of waterways, which in comformation might be likened to a chain, the links of which are as the letter S, we pass from one seeming bayou to another, enclosed, as far as the eye can discover, by an unbroken wall of timber, interlaced with vines in every variety of shade and coloring. Of stream *as such* there is none; at least it is not discernible, and how we are to proceed becomes a query, speedily answered by a torch-light illumination on the upper forward deck, throwing a glare far in advance, revealing to the trusty pilot the (to him) familiar landmarks; pointing our destination, and bringing into strong relief scene after scene, the most weird and gorgeous imaginable.

Outside the radius of the illumination, which distinctly reflects every tree and shrub bordering the stream in the bosom of the little river, the pale moon shines and the stars twinkle; otherwise the gloom is illimitable, and the feeling one of awe, possibly not unmixed with something of superstition, an influence to which the most sceptical are at times susceptible.

A minister is quoting Whittier's lugubrious "Dismal Swamp;" the writer is picturing Dante's mythical river of Death; an old lady tells her traveling companion, "This is my third trip on the Ocklawaha; but I wouldn't miss this for anything."

Ejaculations of pleasure and surprise are heard on every side; and all are lost to everything but the enchantment of the surroundings, when supper is announced, to which we turn with pleasurable anticipations of the luxuries as well as substantials, for which this line is justly famed.

Supper over, all are again assembled on the forward or promenade deck. Anecdotes are told, songs are sung, interspersed with expressions of surprise, pleasure and gratification at every recurring change in the surroundings, and not until Time heralded the approach of another day did we desert our posts. The man of God remarking as he bade the party a cheery "good night," "I have seen many wonders but nothing to compare with this."

Grahamville, seventeen miles below Silver Springs, once the home of the celebrated Seminole, Osceola, is reached at 9 a. m. Eight miles further on we turn into the Silver Spring run, and at 10:30 are at the world famed Silver Spring, the most remarkable body of water on the American continent. Of this enchanting stream one of a party of recent tourists said:

"It has been my good fortune to see some of the most remarkable natural wonders that travelers seek to visit in this country, such as the mountains and glaciers of Alaska, the wonders of Yellowstone Park, the Yosemite valley, the canons of Colorado, the Falls of Niagara, the lakes and rivers of Canada, and the volcanoes of the Hawaiian Islands, and I am free to say that I am glad at last to add the Ocklawaha as a fitting pearl to this long necklace of wonderful jewels."

Silver Springs, the terminus of this line, is the greatest natural curiosity on the American Continent.

"A scene of beauty, such, I ween,
Has seldom been by mortals seen;
The forest dark above, below,
The crystal waters ever flow;
And fa lioms deep, the mai len hair
And sedgy grass is growing there,
Green, with perennial life and tints,
That vary as sunlight glints."

At Silver Springs connection is made via F. C. & P. Railway for all points in the State.

The headquarters of this line are in Palatka.

One of the Hart's Line of Ocklawaha Steamers at Silver Springs.

ANCIENT, COLONIAL AND MODERN. 91

The Southern Express Company.

Students of the marvelous will find much that is interesting, if not seemingly improbable, in the history of the Southern Express Company, one of Florida's most important lines of transportation.
Early in the spring of 1861, Henry B. Plant, then Southern Superintendent of the Adams Express Company, with headquarters at Augusta, Ga., realizing the magnitude of the struggle about to take place between the North and the South, called a meeting of the officers of the Company. The meeting was held at Augusta—now the headquarters of the Southern Express Campany—and was attended by the following named gentlemen, viz: W. B. Dinsmore, President, New York; Edward S. Sanford, General Superintendent, Philadelphia; Alfred Gaitler, Superintendent, Cincinnati, and H. B. Plant, Superintendent, Augusta, Ga. This meeting discussed the situation from the standpoint of practical business, resulting in discontinuance of operations in the Southern States and application to the Superior Court of Georgia for a charter for the "Southern Express Company;" the petitioners being Messrs. John Bones, George T. Jackson, George W. Thew, Henry B. Plant, Francis Whitehead, G. M. Dortie, all of Augusta.

The charter was granted for fourteen years, beginning July 5th, 1861, and the work of organizing and systematizing a force adequate to the necessities of the times at once begun. A Superintendent was placed at Memphis to look after the interests of the company in the West, the appointment falling to Mr. James Shuter. Mr. Edgar C. Hurlbert was made superintendent with headquarters at Atlanta and Mr. Rufus B. Bullock, superintendent, with headquarters at Augusta, Mr. Bullock's division extending to and including Richmond, Va. In the meantime war was declared, and the Southern Express Company was taxed to its utmost carrying capacity, its success marking conspicuously Mr. Plant's extraordinary executive ability.

The great strain on Mr. Plant, President of the Company, mentally and physically, sadly impaired his health, in consequence of which he was forced to take a trip to Europe.

As the war progressed, and the Southern armies moved eastward, the company thought it prudent to move in the same direction, and as a result Atlanta, Ga., received a notable contingent from the west— Mr. M. J. O'Brien exchanging with Mr. Shuter; Mr. O'Brien accepting outside of his many duties as superintendent, the onerous but important office of Commissioner of Exchange for the Southern Confederacy with headquarters at Savannah, Georgia.

The war over and embargoed lines opened, Mr. Plant returned only to find a condition of financial ruin, but his trusted lieutenants, who like the legions of Napoleon, that followed the Eagles of France to Moscow, and ever after boasted that they were the rear guard in the famous retreat, stood at their posts impatient for the herculanean task of rehabilitation.

In this emergency Mr. Plant again assumed active control, and the record of his achievements from that time to the present, forms one of the brightest pages in the history of personal achievement. There is no man, living or dead, who has been a greater factor in building up the South than Henry B. Plant.

THE SOUTHERN EXPRESS COMPANY IN FLORIDA.

To Mr. H. Dempsey, now Superintendent, Augusta, Georgia, belongs the honor of inaugurating the distribution of Express matter in Florida. I quote from a recent letter on the subject:

"I was taken off my run and sent to Florida on important business for the Adams Express Company. This was before the organization of the Southern Express Company in the winter of 1858 and '59.

"My first trip to Florida required a visit to Tallahassee and Jacksonville. I received the freight packages by steamer at Savannah, carried them through the country to Jacksonville, collected charges and made deliveries. I was much pleased with Florida at the time and the people of Florida. They were of the grand old style, and I strongly advocated the entry of the Express lines into Florida.

"The railroad at that time went only as far as Quitman, Ga. I established a line connecting the Georgia and Florida system and the Florida Railroad system. by wagon, between Quitman, Ga., and Madison, Fla "

Following the special mission and recommendation of Mr. Dempsey, the operations of the Southern Express Company were extended to Florida, but owing to want of transportation facilities and limited population, was slow of growth; and it was not until the advent of Mr. C L. Myers, Superintendent, in 1890, with headquarters at Jacksonville that the business assumed anything of its present magnitude. At the present time the company has offices in every city, town and practically every hamlet in the State, and is the most deservedly popular of transportation companies, its name being synonymous with strict regard to the needs of its patrons, integrity, affability and liberality.

In 1875 a renewal of the Company's charter was granted, and in 1886 the Georgia Legislature granted the Company a renewal for thirty years from Dec. 21st, of that year. When the Company was first organized in 1861, Mr. Plant was elected president, and is still in office; the general management of the Company devolving upon Mr. M. J. O'Brien.

It may not be out of place to say of the Southern Express Company that in peace or in war its kindly offices have been appreciated. During the yellow fever epidemics at New Orleans, La.; Memphis and Chattanooga, Tenn; Charleston, S. C.; Savannah and Brunswick, Ga., and Fernandina and Jacksonville, Fla., all supplies for the sufferers were carried free by the Southern Express Company, which did not wait to be asked to perform the service, but solicited contributions from the people, and transported them *free of charge*, and that because of unceasing kindness, its employes are loyal subjects, unalterably devoted to its interests.

This modern giant of traffic organized at Augusta, Ga., in 1861, and nearly annihilated by the war, now embraces every section of the Southern States, south of a line bounded by Norfolk, Richmond, Lynchburg, Roanake, Cincinnati, Columbus, O., Louisville, Owensburg, Evansville, St. Louis, Springfield, Miss., Memphis, Shrevesport New Orleans, and is now one of the strongest and most successful express companies in the western world.

The Southern Express Company covers 24,000 miles of first-class railroad lines; has 2,200 agencies; employs 5,100 persons, 725 of whom are in Florida, and expends annually in Florida, $275,000,

LIST OF OFFICIALS.

H. B. Plant, President, Augusta, Ga., and New York.
M. J O'Brien, Vice-President and General Manager, Augusta, Ga., and New York, N. Y.
M. F. Plant, Vice President, New York, N. Y.
Geo. H. Tilley, Secretary and Treasurer, Augusta, Ga., and New York, N. Y.
C. L. Loop, General Auditor, Chattanooga, Tenn.
T. W. Leary, Assistant General Manager, Chattanooga, Tenn.
Erwin, du Bignon & Chisholm, General Counsel, Savannah, Ga.
New York office, No. 12 West 23d street.

SUPERINTENDENTS.

T. W. Leary, Assistant General Manager, Chattanooga, Tenn.
H. Dempsey, Augusta Division, Augusta, Ga.
C. T. Campbell, Central Division, Chattanooga, Tenn.
O. M. Sadler, Piedmont Division, Charlotte, N. C.
H C. Fisher, Southern Division, Nashville, Tenn.
G. W. Agee, Western Division, Memphis, Tenn.
W. J. Crosswell, Atlantic Division, Wilmington, N. C.
W. W. Hulbert, Georgia Division, Atlanta, Ga.
C. L. Myers, Florida Division, Jacksonville, Fla.
V. Spalding, Eastern Division, Roanoke, Va.
C. A. Pardue, New Orleans, La.

State Officials.

Henry Lawrence Mitchell, Governor.
William D. Bloxham, Comptroller.
John L. Crawford, Secretary of State.
C. B. Collins, Treasurer.
William B. Lamar, Attorney General.
William N. Sheats, State Superintendent of Education.
Patrick Houston, Adjutant General.

SUPREME COURT.

Milton H. Mabry, Chief Justice.
Benjamin S. Liddon, Associate Justice.
R. F. Taylor, Associate Justice.
J. B. Whitfield, Clerk.

CIRCUIT COURT.

FIRST CIRCUIT.
William D. Barnes, Pensacola.

SECOND CIRCUIT.
John W. Malone, Quincy.

THIRD CIRCUIT.
John F. White, Live Oak.

FOURTH CIRCUIT.
Rhydon M. Call, of Jacksonville.

FIFTH CIRCUIT.
William A. Hocker, of Ocala.

SIXTH CIRCUIT.
Barron Phillips, Tampa.

SEVENTH CIRCUIT.
John D. Broome, DeLand.

JUDGES OF CRIMINAL COURTS OF RECORD.

Escambia County.

John C. Avery, Pensacola.

Duval County.
H. B. Phillips, Jacksonville.

Putnam County.
Robert W. Davis, Palatka.

Marion County.
William S. Bullock, Ocala.

Hillsboro County.
Gen. J. B. Wall, Tampa.

Lake County.
J. B. Gaines.

Orange County.
Cecil G. Butt.

Volusia County.
J. A. Stewart, DeLand.

U. S. DISTRICT JUDGES.

Northern District—Chas. Swayne.
Southern District—Jas. W. Locke.

ROSTER OF NATIONAL GUARD—FLORIDA, WITH DATE OF RANK.

Gov. Henry L. Mitchell. Commander-in-Chief, Tallahassee.
Major-General Patrick Houston, Adjutant-General, Tallahassee.
ON THE GENERAL STAFF.
Col. D. E. Maxwell, Assistant Adjutant-General, Fernandina.
Col. Frank Phillips, Quartermaster-General, Marianna.
Col. F. A. Salomonson, Commissary-General, Tampa.
Col. Evans Haile, Judge Advocate-General, Gainesville.
Col. D. G. Brent, Inspector-General, Pensacola.
Col. Henry Bacon, Surgeon General, Jacksonville.
ON THE PERSONAL STAFF.
Col. T. C. Taliaferro. Aide-de Camp, Tampa.
Capt. L. J. Brumby, Aide-de Camp, Ocala.
FIRST BATTALION.
Headquarters Jacksonville, Florida.
Major M. P. Turner, commanding, June 23, 1893.
1st Lieutenant E. W. Vail, Adjutant, July 21, 1893.

1st Lieutenant C. H. Chesnut, Quartermaster and Commissary, July 21, 1893.
1st Lieutenant L. Alexander, Surgeon, St. Augustine.

Co. A, Jacksonville Light Infantry, Jacksonville, Fla.
Capt. W. J. Driscoll, commanding, June 12, 1894.
1st Lieutenant B. B. MacDonell, November 27, 1894.
2d Lieutenant J. S. Maxwell, November 27, 1894.
Co. B, St. Augustine Guards, St. Augustine, Fla.
Capt. F. H. Greatorex, commanding, July 18, 1892.
1st Lieutenant A. J. Pallicer, Jr., August 22, 1893.
2d Lieutenant M. T. Masters, August 22, 1893.
Co. C, Metropolitan Light Infantry, Jacksonville, Fla.
Capt. L. H. Mattair, commanding, July 29, 1891.
1st Lieutenant James Y. Wilson, July 24, 1894.
2d Lieutenant John W. Kennedy, July 24, 1894.
Co. D, St. Augustine Rifles, St. Augustine, Fla.
Capt. J. W. Brannon, commanding, January 23, 1891.
1st Lieuteant Theo. V. Pomar, December 11, 1891.
2d Lieutenant F. J. Howatt, July 21, 1893.
Co. F, Wilson Battery, Jacksonville, Fla.
Capt. J. Gumbinger, commanding, March 2, 1894.
1st Lieutenant C. M. Smith, January, 1895.

SECOND BATTALION.
Headquarters Leesburg, Florida.
Major C. P. Lovell, commanding, August 17, 1893.
1st Lieutenant J. N. Bradshaw, Adjutant, July 23, 1894.
1st Lieutenant   Quartermaster Commissary.
1st Lieutenant R. P. Izlar, Surgeon, June 30, 1892.

Co. A, Ocala Rifles, Ocala, Fla.
Capt. R. E. Davidson, commanding, February 13, 1894.
1st Lieutenant R. T. Biedsey, February 13, 1894.
2d Lieutenant J. W. Lancaster, February 13, 1894.
Co. B, Leesburg Rifles, Leesburg, Fla.
Capt. George E. Lovell, commanding, March 23, 1894.
1st Lieutenant J. C. West, July 26, 1894.
2d Lieutenant J. Charles Hall, July 26, 1894.
Co. C, Shine Guards, Orlando, Fla.
Capt. Philip B. Bewan, commanding, January 3, 1894.
1st Lieutenant William H. Reynolds, March 17, 1894.
2d Lieutenant Albert Winston Scruggs, March 17, 1894.
Co. D, Gate City Rifles, Sanford, Fla.
Capt. Charles D. Leffler, commanding, January 14, 1892.
1st Lieutenant W. D. Miller, July 28, 1892.
2d Lieutenant A. P. Hockstein, July 28, 1892.

ANCIENT, COLONIAL AND MODERN. 97

THIRD BATTALION.

Headquarters Pensacola, Florida.

Major W. F. Williams, commanding, July 21, 1887.
1st Lieutenant F. A. Ross, Adjutant, July 10, 1893.
1st Lieutenant S. B. Hutchinson, Quartermaster and Commissary, August 3, 1893.
1st Lieutenant R. W. Hargis, Surgeon, July 21, 1887.

Co. A, Escambia Rifles, Pensacola, Fla.
  Capt. R. M. Bushnell, commanding, November 24, 1893.
  1st Lieutenant J. K. Hyer, November 24, 1893.
  2d Lieutenant S. J. Gonzalez, November 24, 1893.
Co. B, Chipley Light Infantry, Pensacola, Fla.
  Capt. R. M. Cary, Jr., commanding, February 15, 1894.
  1st Lieutenant W. S. Oerting, February 15, 1894.
  2d Lieutenant
Co. C, Franklin Rifles, Appalachicola, Fla.
  Capt. P. S. Hickey, commanding, August 19, 1892.
  1st Lieutenant A. S. Mohr, August 19, 1892.
  2d Lieutenant J. P. Lovell, August 19, 1892.
Co. D, Suwanee Rifles, Live Oak, Fla.
  Capt. L. K. Kimmerlin, commanding, Nov. 25, 1893.
  1st Lieutenant E. G. Allen, November 25, 1893.
  2d Lieutenant R. H. Haddock, November 25, 1893.
Co. F, Pensacola Light Artillery, Pensacola, Fla.
  Capt. M. P. Palmes, commanding, August 17, 1891.
  1st Lieutenant A. H. D'Alemberte, August 5, 1893.

FOURTH BATTALION.

Headquarters Gainesville, Florida.

Major Irving E. Webster, commanding, May 30, 1892.
1st Lieutenant Walter M. Davis, Adjutant, December 4, 1891.
1st Lieutenant C. M. Bingham, Jr., Quartermaster and Commissary, June 17, 1892.
1st Lieutenant E. L. Stewart, Surgeon, January 17, 1892.

Co. A, Fernaudina Guards, Fernandina, Fla.
  Capt. A. Baushell, commanding, August 1, 1894.
  1st Lieutenant J. C. Angel, August 1, 1894.
  2d Lieutenant George E. Willis, August 1, 1894.
Co. B, Bradford County Guards, Starke, Fla.
  Capt. R. C. Heiberger, commanding, April 21, 1890.
  1st Lieutenant O. C. Husband, March 30, 1894.
  2d Lieutenant O. G. Husband, March 30, 1894.
Co. C, Gem City Guards, Palatka, Fla.
  Capt. H. M. DeMontmollin, commanding, December 4, 1893.
  1st Lieutenant J. Stewart Lewis, July 18, 1894.

98 GLIMPSES OF FLORIDA:

  2d Lieutenant Jesse E. Burtz, July 18, 1894.
Co. D, Halifax Rifles, Daytona, Fla.
  Capt. J. S. Herbert, commanding, May 15, 1893.
  1st Lieutenant Jerome D. Maley, May 15, 1893.
  2d Lieutenant W. H. Carter, June 8, 1892.

FIFTH BATTALION.
Headquarters Tampa, Florida.

  Major Douglas F. Conoley, commanding, July 23, 1894.
  1st Lieutenant I. D. Craft, Adjutant, August 30, 1892.
  1st Lieutenant Albert F. Shultz, Quartermaster and Commissary April 10, 1894.
  1st Lieutenant J. B. Maloney, Surgeon, August 15, 1892.

Co. A, Island City Guards, Key West, Fla.
  Capt. F. C. Brossier, commanding, June 6, 1888.
  1st Lieutenant M. W. Curry, June 25, 1892.
  2d Lieutenant H. L. Roberts, June 10, 1890.
Co. B, Tampa Rifles, Tampa, Fla.
  Capt. Charles C. Whitaker, commanding, August 3, 1894.
  1st Lieutenant Frank Burke, August 3, 1894.
  2d Lieutenant Fred W. Krause, August 3, 1894.
Co. C, Indian River Guards, Titusville, Fla.
  Capt. Arthur T. Feaster, commanding, February 26, 1894.
  1st Lieutenant J. T. Sanders, February 26, 1894.
  2d Lieutenant J. C. Jones, February 26, 1894.
Co. D, DeSoto Guards, Arcadia, Fla.
  Capt. Charles W. Forrester, commanding, December 14, 1893.
  1st Lieutenant E. T. Smith, December 14, 1893.
  2d Lieutenant F. Lutzens, December 14, 1893.
State Troops number about 900.

SOME OF THE LEADING HOTELS OF FLORIDA.

WINDSOR HOTEL.
JOHN E. BAKER and OWEN TRAVERS, Props.   JACKSONVILLE, FLORIDA.

THE INN
PORT TAMPA, FLORIDA.

J. H. KING,
MANAGER PLANT SYSTEM HOTELS.
TAMPA BAY HOTEL, TAMPA,
THE INN, PORT TAMPA,
THE SEMINOLE, WINTER PARK, FLA.

OCALA HOUSE.

The capital of one of the richest counties in Florida (Marion), has been dubbed "The Brick City," the hub of Agriculture, Horticulture and Commerce. The enterprise and push of its business men remind one of the vigorous Western cities.

The Ocala House is the finest between Palatka and Punta Gorda, embodying in its general arrangement the best modern ideas of comfort and safety. Ocala enjoys excellent transportation facilities; is on the line of the Florida Southern Railroad, 71 miles south of Palatka, and is reached direct, via the Tropical Trunk Line and F. C. & P. Rty.

PRINTING

BINDING

RULING

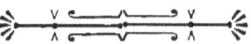

DaCosta Printing Co.

Jacksonville.

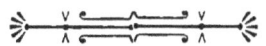

COMMERCIAL

BOOK and JOB

RAILROAD

www.ingramcontent.com/pod-product-compliance
Lightning Source LLC
Chambersburg PA
CBHW020132170426
43199CB00010B/725